The Art of Persian Cooking

The Art of Persian Cooking

Forough-es-Saltaneh Hekmat

HIPPOCRENE BOOKS
New York

Hippocrene paperback edition, 1994.
Third printing, 2005.

Copyright © 1961 Doubleday & Company, Inc.

For information, address:
HIPPOCRENE BOOKS, INC.
171 Madison Avenue
New York, NY 10016

ISBN 0-7818-0241-5

Printed in the United States of America.

This book is dedicated to Dr. Albert H. Domm, of Los Angeles, who restored me to health; to the many American friends who urged me to write it, and to my country, Iran, which inspired the unique cuisine and poetry presented herewith.

Contents

Preface

During the nine years that I lived in the United States of America I watched with pleasure the curiosity and interest of my friends in Berkeley, San Francisco, Los Angeles, and New York as they enjoyed the exotic and delicate Persian dishes I served to them. It was their urging that persuaded me to commit my knowledge of Persian cooking to paper.

Increased communications and extensive travel from one country to another have made a pygmy of our world to a point where all men are neighbors. Today there is more need than ever before for all people to work together toward a mutual understanding of the customs, manners, and morals of other lands and cultures.

Certainly one fundamental of life that all men have in common is food. Everyone must eat to survive, but different people have different food preferences and various methods of preparing their dishes. To understand the food habits and tastes of another country enables one to understand more fully that people's way of life.

Since food is generally based on tradition, I believe that to learn only the recipes of a country's classic dishes is not sufficient. Some knowledge of the traditions behind the dishes, or at least some details of their historical and cultural origins, seems desirable. However, to compress the traditions of a nation like Persia, whose customs have changed constantly throughout the ages, is beyond the capacity of any one book. Despite the difficulties I have attempted in this book to depict typical customs of Iranian life, along with descriptions of traditional concepts of culinary art which, though dating back to ancient times, are still in existence today.

For many centuries the Iranians have looked upon food from three different points of view—the medicinal, the philosophical, and the cultural. Their physicians and philosophers considered food and drink as the principal factors in reviving the body and as an effective means to strengthen or weaken man's character. Consuming an excess of rich and luxurious foods, such as enormous quantities of red meats, fats, starch, or alcoholic beverages, was considered to provoke evil thoughts and to convert a man into a greedy, selfish beast. A healthful diet of vegetables, fruits, fish, fowl, and certain delicacies composed of mixed petals and blossoms of roses was believed to have unusual powers that could transform man into a gentle and noble creature.

> *Eat naught but regal food,*
> *If you would develop both the body and the soul.*

This bit of wisdom was penned by an ancient Persian philosopher.

Short explanations of some of the foods and beverages believed to be the most constructive to health, because of their medicinal values, are given in the last chapter of this book.

The third point of view is the cultural and artistic. Food was considered an art, furnishing enjoyment to both body and mind. And so the Iranians cultivated not only the taste and flavor of their dishes, but the manner in which they were presented. Unfortunately most of the elaborately artistic and outstanding dishes in Persian classical cooking have never been recorded. In the course of the ages they have been passed down orally or visually from generation to generation and, as usual, each family proudly cooks its inherited recipes for its own enjoyment.

Not only do Persian dishes vary from one section of the country to another—just as, in China, Cantonese cuisine differs from Peking cooking—but from family to family. In general the peerage of Shiraz has always been famous throughout Persia for exceptional skill in the culinary arts, and many of the recipes in this book are from Shiraz, handed down to me by my grandmothers and members of my family on both sides who, generation after generation, produced these same dishes in their kitchens for various public offerings and for private parties. It was in Shiraz, a thirteenth-century city in southern Iran, where I was born. It is close to Persepolis, the ancient capital of Persia.

To supplement these recipes, I have translated and tested many others which I have gathered for years from my friends of big, old families living in the greatest cities in the north, east, and west of the country.

Now nothing more of importance remains for me to say except to offer my sincere thanks to my dear friend, Miss Franses Richardson of Los Angeles, the intelligent and learned head of the library of Twentieth Century Fox, who favored me by reading and commenting upon the composition of this book with great honesty; to His Excellency, Mr. Pahlbod, General Director of General Administration of Fine Arts of Iran and to Dr. Simin Daneshvar, Editor of *Nagsho-Negar,* the periodical by the Administration of Fine Arts, who granted me permission to reproduce the old paintings and pictures in this book. Their help was indispensable.

F.H.

April, 1959   Los Angeles

Haft Seen—Seven S'es, in a middle class family at the time of New Year. The items I have talked about in the book—especially the green grass in the center—are shown here. The young man is looking at his watch, heralding the arrival of the New Year. The other man is reciting from the Qoran at that particular moment.

Part One

CHAPTER I

The History of Persian Cooking

as Reflected in Persian Feasts and
Special Occasions.

Wake up, O Drowsy One!
Depart from your pillow of neglect.
Look at the Market of Life,
How many substances there are
To strengthen your being.
To neglect them makes you a picture on the wall!

Bos-hac—Thirteenth century

Persian literature is as richly beautiful as her hand-woven rugs, silks, brocades, delicately worked jewelry, miniatures, and magnificent architecture. It is equally enriched by poetic references to Persia's culinary art, which the Iranians, by means of their artistic skill, elevated to a high degree, producing many masterpieces and delicacies.

Firdausi, the great Persian epic writer, tells an enchanting tale about a knight who was captured and imprisoned in a deep well by the enemy king of a neighboring country; whereupon Rostram, the famous hero, accompanied by a thousand followers, went secretly to the enemy's land to rescue him. Arriving there, he ordered a chicken to be cooked and stuffed with rare ingredients. Then, putting his ring in the center of the stuffing, he sent it as a gift to the hopeless prisoner. Thus word was conveyed that Rostram had come to the rescue.

There are many other such stories in which food or drink plays an important role.

About 700 years ago a poet, Bos-hac of Shiraz, wrote a book of satirical lyrics, calling his characters by the names of different foods and beverages. By means of these symbolic characters he narrated critical observations on the political situation of his time. Using the same food-named characters, he went on to pen many of his own philosophical ideas. In one he says:

*O Loaf of Sugar! Enjoy not the melting of plain sugar
into water,
For your own fate will certainly be the same.
Do not be grieved, O Sour Orange! Like the sweet orange,
turn into preserves
And then your sourness will change into sweetness.
Ah, how sad! It seems we cannot have apricots, I muttered
to my Heart.
Despair not, at least there is watermelon,
My Heart consoled me.
O Quince, would you wish to associate with the sincere
and the honest,
Throw off your woolen mantle of hypocrisy and run away
even from yourself.
Just as no one, so far, knows the inner secret of the watermelon.
Each has a sweet dream of his own!*

Artistically combined foods have played a major role in the
life of the Persian people. History has preserved numerous
records of social and political events wherein food played a
part. They tell how crimes were committed by means of delicious foods, temptingly displayed. Many kings, amirs, and
other dignitaries were poisoned by a *halva* prepared by a queen
or a slavemaid. But more often *halva* played a peaceful role
in settling differences between two or more people. Bos-hac
wrote wisely:

> *We brought halva for peace,
> Never mind if there is a fight between it and the
> sugar pilou.*

As might be expected, women have had a great influence on
the cookery of Iran. Thousands of recipes have been devised
by Persian women. In the palaces of Persian kings there have
always been women who, though plain of feature, have been
held in highest esteem, frequently displacing in favor the

most ravishing court beauties because of their incredible skill in the preparation of food. Even the average housewife was aware that carefully prepared food was appreciated, and she took pride in her work.

Consequently, home-cooked food in Iran far outclasses in delicacy and flavor any dishes prepared in the inns or eating places.

Throughout the ages the influence of Persian culinary art spread to all the Middle Eastern countries—to Turkey, Iraq, Armenia, and Syria—where today these same dishes are prepared, but they all have their origin deeply rooted in the culinary history of Persia.

As in other countries, the people of Iran have special dishes for special occasions. Through the ages their culinary traditions have been faithfully observed at weddings, birthdays, and funerals; at religious and historical feasts as well as at many formal and state gatherings.

A PERSIAN HOME

At a traditional Persian banquet in a private home or in the mosques, the best of foods and refreshments is set aside to be served to the public and the poor with the compliments of the host. This custom from olden times is observed today even in small towns by the aristocracy and the well-to-do-merchant class, many of whom still maintain two separate houses, each close to the other. The first, called the *andarooni* (inner house), was set aside especially for the women of the family. The second, the *birooni* (outside house) was dedicated to the head of the family, the aga, and his sons and menservants. Most of the aga's time, until late at night, was passed in the *birooni*, while he attended to his business and received friends, often serving lunch to them. If guests were present at noon-time, it was considered mandatory for the aga to offer food. Letting a friend or acquaintance leave one's house hungry is still considered the height of discourtesy.

At the same time the women, together with their maidserv-ants, had their own friends in to lunch in the *andarooni*. But preparing meals for both houses was and still is the responsi-bility of the matriarch, or *khanom* of the house, who gives the orders to the cook.

Both houses were completely walled, and the flower gardens, the carefully tended trees, and a pool of fresh water were all part of the enclosed courtyard. Between the pool and the flower beds the ground was paved with large bricks, and on summer afternoons carpets were spread on these bricks and chairs and tables set out for the heads of the two houses and their friends. Such is still the general style of the houses, either large or small, rich or poor. But it is in the more sumptuous dwellings that many of the public feasts always have taken place.

THE MARRIAGE CEREMONY IN IRAN

One of the most important social functions, even among the lesser-known families, is the wedding reception. According to historical records, many ancient wedding customs remained all over the country as the most important part of the marriage until almost twenty years ago. These ceremonies still exist in all parts of Iran, either as they were in olden times or with slight modifications.

One of the oldest traditions is that all the delicacies for the wedding must be prepared by the women at home, so many of the women who are close relatives and friends of the engaged couple gather together in the houses of both the bride and the groom during the month preceding the ceremonial days of the wedding. There they make a large number of special and elaborate pastries and sweetmeats. The quantity, of course, depends on the number of guests anticipated, but generally more sweets than are required are made so that they may be sent to friends and relatives who are unable to attend the feast and given to the servants who help prepare the feast.

The Engagement Day

In former days all the women relatives and friends of the couple were invited to lunch at the bride's home by her mother, to announce the engagement. A diamond ring, a large Cashmere shawl, large trays of a special wedding candy called *noqle*, and a bowl made of sugar candy were presented to the bride by the groom's mother or sisters. All sorts of cookies, candies, nuts named *ajeel*, fruit, tea, and other refreshing beverages or sherbets were served by the bride's mother.

Today the engagement celebration is limited to an afternoon party and the guests limited to the close relatives and friends of both families. *Noqle* and *ajeel*, however, are special treats for this happy occasion, and their recipes are given in a later chapter.

The Matrimonial Ceremony

The wedding day is the most important one for the Iranian Moslem women. Prominent personalities known to the family are invited to sign the marriage certificate, or *gabaaleh*, which is the agreement of the dowry, or *mahr*. The *mahr* outlines the amount of money, villages, houses, and gardens, or any other such property which is settled on the bride by the groom. In some Moslem countries the amount is insignificant, but in Iran it is a very costly business. It is a form of protection for Moslem women against divorce, the right of which is given to the man. If he wants to divorce his wife, he is obliged to pay the whole amount of the property agreed upon according to the *gabaaleh*. In cases where the wife wishes a divorce, she may absolve her husband from payment of her dowry.

The following beautiful traditions and customs are still followed everywhere among Iranian Moslem families:

At the time arranged for the actual matrimonial ceremony, which is almost always in the afternoon, the bride sits in front of a large gold- or silver-framed mirror. At the sides of the mirror are two gold, silver, or crystal candlesticks, lighted with colored candles. The mirror and candlesticks are presents from the groom, symbolizing the happiness and purity awaiting the bride's future life with him. On her knee is an open volume of the sacred Qoran, while masses of beautifully colored and fragrant flowers surround her. From head to toe she is covered with a gold-embroidered net veil, and a square of Cashmere shawl, embroidered with gold and real pearls, called a prayer rug, is spread in front of her. Large gilded trays are placed on each side of the rug, and on the trays are arranged large pieces of white cheese, fresh, green, aromatic herbs, and a special flat bread on which a poem of blessing and prosperity is written in colored sesame seeds. The cheese, greens, and bread are shared with the guests after the ceremony as a symbol of prosperity.

The air is scented by burning incense, and the bride sits silently while two Moslem priests, representing both the bride and the groom, recite prayers. Then the priest representing the bride asks her consent.

"Young, noble, honest, and matured lady, are you willing to marry this honorable man?"

Then he mentions the amount of the *mahr*.

Three times he asks the same question, but there is no answer from the bride until the third time. It is at the moment when she says "yes" that she and the groom become legally man and wife.

During this ceremony three happily married women play a part. Two hold a square of white silk over the bride's head, while the other rubs two large pieces of lump sugar together, making a shower of sugar on the silk. This action symbolizes the happiness and sweetness that will be the bride's in her married life.

After saying "yes," the bride is kissed on the forehead by the groom and is presented with a gold ring and a wedding gift consisting of a piece of jewelry. Then she is kissed by her parents and the groom's parents and is showered with *noqle* mixed with pearls and with gold or silver coins. The pearls and coins are gathered by the guests as souvenirs.

As a rule the matrimonial ceremonies are held in the bride's home, and tea, other beverages, fruit, *ajeel,* and *noqle* and other homemade pastries are served. Then comes a happy interval between the wedding ceremony and the actual wedding night, during which time traditions important to the Iranians are diligently observed by all families, rich or poor.

One of these is the dowry, or *jahiz,* presented to the bride by her parents. The amount of the *jahiz* generally depends on the amount of the *mahr*—the more the *mahr* agreed upon by the groom, the more the *jahiz,* which consists of all the necessities for a new home, including furniture, carpets, draperies, chandeliers, mirrors, kitchen appliances, et cetera. In former days such items as large silver bowls and jugs were given to the groom for washing his face and hands, and brooms, the handles embroidered with gold and real pearls, were included among the gifts for sweeping the bride's rooms. Other expensive gifts of clothing and jewelry for the bridegroom, his parents and brothers and sisters and fabrics or money for the servants were also part of the *jahiz,* which often required from two to six months to complete.

Another tradition, which is still customary in many parts of Iran, is a shower for the groom, but not, as in America, for the bride. About a week before the wedding the elders of the town or village gather together, and each presents the young groom with money, or if the groom is a farmer, the gifts may consist of a couple of cows, mules, or seeds for cultivation.

Taking the couple to the public bath was another happy and popular ceremony. The custom still exists in some parts of the country. On the day before the wedding night the bride and groom, riding on horseback, were each taken to separate public baths by their relatives. At the head of this happy procession were musicians and men carrying torches flaming with perfumed oil. After the washing was over, the happy caravan returned home.

On the afternoon of the actual wedding night the bride's mother again entertained the women relatives and friends of both families at her home, and again sherbets, *noqle*, *ajeel*, and fruits were served. After the repast all the guests followed the bride to her new home for the nuptial night. The bride rode either on horseback or in a decorated carriage called a "moving throne," carried by four horses or mules. The interior of the carriage was decorated with puffed satin cushions and draperies. Once more groups of musicians led the parade while servants carrying flaming, musk-perfumed torches and jingling crystal candlesticks illuminated the path. The bride entered her new home via a pathway paved with flowers, symbolizing her new life of freshness and beauty.

For a specified three to seven days women guests stayed at the inner house with the bride, and their meals included breakfasts of pastries, white cheese, tea, and fruit, as well as many elaborate and costly special dishes for luncheons and dinners.

Men friends and relatives stayed at the outer house with the groom and his father, only for the wedding evening. After dinner and beverages, served from ten o'clock until midnight, everyone went home.

Public wedding feasts took place at the groom's home either three to seven days before or after the wedding night. The number of these feasts depended upon the wealth, social position, or importance of the families of the bride and groom.

On the morning after the wedding night a great shower of gifts poured in from parents, friends, and acquaintances. The gifts from the mothers and fathers were always very special— bracelets, necklaces, rings and brooches of diamonds, emeralds, rubies, and pearls, and a written deed to a house or garden or part of some property. This custom still exists all over the country.

When my sister and I were married, each of us was given half of a village. Formerly gifts were delivered by servants and were taken first into the presence of the groom's mother. After that they were taken to the room of the bride, in the house of the groom's father.

Since Iranian women officially set aside the veil, over twenty years ago, and took their place beside men in the social world, many of these customs have been gradually changing. The younger generation has become Westernized to some extent, and families are not as wealthy as they once were. No one stays for a week at the wedding house, as in former days, and often a party given at a hotel takes the place of all the feastings and celebrations of old.

THE BIRTH OF A BABY

Next in importance to a wedding as a reason for celebration is the birth of a child. While still an important occasion in Iran today, the ceremonies are greatly changed.

Formerly dinners and luncheons were served to relatives and

friends. Women were entertained in the *andarooni* by the ladies of the household, and men were entertained in the *birooni* by the father. On the seventh night after the birth of the baby a large dinner and reception were given to all. On that night, for about two hours before dinner, the baby, dressed in its best clothes, was passed from one elderly and important lady of rank or age to another, sitting side by side on the sofas, chanting the following hymn:

"Hold the baby; pass the baby; God protects the baby."

After that the mullah (priest) who had been invited to officiate would come in to recite the prayer and name the child. Plenty of cookies, special candies, pastries, fruit, and nuts—almonds, pistachios, and fruit seeds—were served both before and after dinner. In many families the guests were entertained with music and singing which continued through the night. On the following day all the leftover food was distributed to the servants and others who had labored to prepare the feast. A considerable number of poor families, too, were served the elaborate dishes special to such occasions. At the present time these ceremonies are reduced to one or two large dinners, given sometime after the birth of the child.

THE NEW YEAR (*Nowrooze*)

Since 8699 years ago, as shown in the Zoroastrian calendar, Iranians have had their national festivities on the arrival of each of the four seasons of the year, but the greatest of these is the beginning of spring, March 21 to 22. This is our New Year, and it is as old and magnificent as the history of Iran itself.

Nowrooze, as it is called, means "New Day." It begins the moment the sun passes the sign Aries in the vernal equinox in March. In ancient times the New Day celebrations continued for forty days, and the entire time was spent in music, dancing, games, and visiting. They were days of great happiness for all but those who were in mourning, and everyone was excused from paying any taxes during those holidays. Today the celebration lasts for only thirteen days, but many of the old customs still remain.

During the month preceding Nowrooze a thorough cleaning takes place inside and outside the house. The furniture is rearranged and all the carpets are washed and cleaned. Garden pools are cleaned, and new flowers and plants replenish the flower beds. In the kitchen, too, there is great activity. The ladies attend to the making of a multitude of sweetmeats appropriate for the occasion, and a particular sweet bread for the New Day is prepared by women specialists, who come to stay in the houses for several days and nights to make it.

History relates that in ancient Persia, at the first moment of the transition to the new year, all the products of the earth available in the country had to be presented to the shah, (king) by all the different classes of the people in a special ceremony.

The most beautiful girl of the court, magnificently costumed, presented the shah with a large tray of gold on which was placed a token of all the commodities of the country.

"What have you brought to me?" the shah asked.
"I have brought you happiness," the girl replied.
"Where have you come from?" he queried.
"From the land of happiness," she answered.
"What do you want?" he questioned.
"Prosperity and joy for all, up to the End."

At that moment, by the order of the shah, the rubies, pearls, diamonds, and other precious gems which had been hung in huge bunches on the cypress and date trees surrounding the reception chamber were presented to the people. The trees themselves had been covered from top to bottom with large leaves of gold.

By the same token, presentations were made to the grandees, nobles, and landowners by their subjects. This official royal checking of the economic situation of the country became a national ceremony of Nowrooze and is continued today in all families.

In the houses of both large and small families the table is the highlight of the happy moment when the sun passes to the sign Aries in March. The table, called *haft seen,* meaning "the seven S's," is spread with a white cloth called a *sofreh* and decorated with the products of man and nature—all sorts of vegetables, meats, fowl, fish, dairy products, eggs, both raw and cooked, sweetmeats and pastries, all manner of nuts, grains, and cereals. Also put upon the table are fresh water, salt, flowers, a mirror, and lighted candles. Each of these items is symbolic. The special flowers for the table are violets, hyacinths, and narcissuses. Young, green blades of wheat and lentils are other important and traditional items placed upon the table. About twenty days before Nowrooze raw wheat and lentils are soaked and left to grow into a mass of greenery. Then a clay jar covered with these green shoots must be there for each member of the family, as a symbol of the roots of his life.

These verdant jars are most attractive at the table. On top of each is fixed a lighted white wax candle, decorated with red, green, and gold designs. The children's nurses and the servants used to prepare the jars, the decorative candles, also oranges decorated with artificial gold leaf, and would bring them as presents to the lady of the house who would, in turn, present them with other gifts of money or expensive fabrics and plenty of sweetmeats.

As the old year gave way to the new, the mother of the

family extinguished the candles with two green leaves or small white candies.

A special sweet, rich, brown halva called *samanie*, made with wheat flour and water and containing quantities of walnuts and almonds, is traditional at the New Day table. There are many references in Persian literature to this delicacy.

From the first moment of the New Year all the members of the family gather around the *haft seen*, waiting for the old year to give way to the new. If, for any reason, a member of the family is absent, his or her picture is there instead. Past unhappinesses, anxieties, and conflicts are forgotten; if not, the person must carry the burden of these unfriendly feelings for another entire year.

The arrival of Nowrooze is symbolized by an ancient superstition whereby a few eggs placed on a mirror on the table seem to move slightly. According to Persian mythology, the earth was placed on one horn of a mythological bull who lives on the back of an enormous whale in the sea beneath the seventh stratum of the earth. Once a year, at the moment of the New Year, the bull, tired of carrying weight on one horn, moves the earth from one horn to the other. The eggs, symbolic of the earth, supposedly move to indicate the movement of the earth being transferred to a new horn. It is a moment of great rejoicing, kissing, and embracing.

An amusing part of the New Year celebration is that a mother must eat as many cooked and dyed eggs as she has children. Even those mothers who never eat eggs at any other time try to manage it. But I cannot remember that my mother ever managed to eat more than two eggs, even though she had seven children!

Another folk legend connected with the New Year's activities is an interesting one worth recounting. Tradition relates that Nowrooze is personified by *Babaa-Nowrooze*, meaning

Old-Father-New-Day, and he is represented with a long white beard and a hoary head. Ten days before his arrival, when new life begins to awaken on earth, Mother Old (Nani-Now-rooze), who is waiting for him, prepares everything so that it will be clean, fresh, and beautiful—washes, sweeps, dusts, cooks, and cleans the whole world. Then, being very tired, she takes a nap. Just at this moment Baba comes and goes. Waking, Mother Old finds she has missed him.

"Ah, he is gone, gone! I will take a flame and burn the whole world!"

And she becomes so furious that she picks up a flaming piece of wood and throws it onto the earth. The whole world turns into flames! And the hot summer begins.

The chicken, vegetables, and fish which decorate the *haft seen* table are used to make the *Nowrooze polou,* a rice dish which is served either on the first night or the first day of the Nowrooze. The recipe will be given in a later chapter. Relatives, friends, and servants are all invited to the polou meal.

It is also the custom that, a week before Nowrooze, live chickens, eggs, fresh fruit, yogurt and other dairy products are brought to the house of the landlord from his villages. Great portions of these commodities are distributed among the servants with pounds and pounds of rice and purified butter for them to make a *Nowrooze polou* in their own houses for their families.

All the old families, including my maternal and paternal families, were most particular about carrying out every phase of this very special tradition.

On the very first morning of Nowrooze the festivities begin, and receptions and visits to friends are continued for thirteen days, during which time all schools and public offices are closed throughout the country. It is the custom for the youngest and

those of inferior station to visit their elders and those of importance in the community first. The elders and important citizens
repay the visit at a later date. Even slight aquaintances visit
one another, and on these visits gifts, mostly gold and silver
coins, are given to the young by the adult.

On the thirteenth day, the last day of the Nowrooze festivities, which traditionally is supposed to be an unlucky day, all
people, rich and poor, enjoy an all-day picnic. This last day
must be observed away from home, with all sorts of fun, games,
music, dancing, and the enjoyment of quantities of food and
beverages. The food of this day is kababs served with wine,
ajeel, and special sweetmeats.

DEATH

Another important occasion when food plays a role in the
traditions of our country is at the time of mourning for the
dead. Formerly these ceremonies lasted from three to seven
days. At the present time they are limited to three days only.

During this time friends and relatives gather in the house of
the deceased to console the family. There are specific foods,
desserts, and halvas for these occasions. At the same time whole
meals, with halva and fruits, are distributed to the poor.

On the afternoon of the seventh day the mourners, accompanied by both men and women relatives and friends, visit the
cemetery. Carpets are spread on the grave and on them are
placed crystal candlesticks with lighted candles, china vases
filled with flowers, and large dishes of sweetmeats, fruits, and
halvas. Coffee, the beverage served on mourning occasions,
is served to everyone.

After sitting for an hour on the carpets and quietly reading
prayers, the mourners retire to a room to listen to the mullah,
(priest) who recites prayers and relates the tragic stories of the

Prophet and his family which offer consolation to the bereaved. Then they return home, and the candles, flowers, and foods are distributed to the poor. The same ceremony is repeated on the fortieth day after death, and from then on mourning is over until one year has passed. On this day the seventh-day ceremony is repeated.

A special kind of halva, made of either sugar or dates, is always served to the poor during these ceremonies. In olden days, these halvas were put in a large bowl and carried behind the bier of the deceased. Bos-hac has this to say:

> *What of a basin of halva, carried behind my bier tomorrow,*
> *While hunger ends me in disgrace today?*

PUBLIC RELIGIOUS OFFERINGS

The religion of Islam has developed the natural generosity of the people of Iran. The offering of food and refreshments to the public, and especially to the poor, is an expression of that generosity. Public feasts, served in private houses or in the mosques, are paid for by wealthy hosts and hostesses.

There are two different occasions when food is offered to the public. The first is purely for charity's sake, and the offering is given at any time of the year by one person or, in these days, more often by a group. The second is a religious ceremony which takes place on the specific days or nights of the mourning months of Muharram and Safar (the first and second months of the Arabic year) and on the fasting month of Ramadan (the ninth month of the Arabic year).

All charity dinners used to be free. No one ever paid for them. But since the inhabitants of the big cities have become Westernized, some of them consider free charity feedings old-fashioned. Now they gather in groups, arrange a party, serve the food, but sell tickets to help the poor.

Still, free charity receptions are the custom to some extent all over the country. They may be offered in thankfulness for the recovery of the health of a beloved child or relative, for the success of a difficult business or financial enterprise, or to express gratitude for the birth of a long-wanted child. For any of these reasons and many more, the best of food is offered to the poor, and the feasts last from one to three nights, depending on the importance of the subject or the wealth of the benefactor.

Religious public feastings, on the other hand, commemorate either happy or sad events in the life of the prophet Mohammed and his family, such as his birthday, the birthday of any of his twelve descendants (Imams), or the day he was elected by God as His Apostle Messenger (*Payghambar*), which is a happy occasion for Moslems. Among the faithful observers of these events are many aristocrats and wealthy businessmen, who hold the celebrations at their houses, as well as at the bazaars, mosques or at Hosainiyehs. Hosainiyehs are large houses dedicated to Iman Hussein by wealthy men and women for public feasts. They have vast grounds and gardens where the people sit and are served.

When there is a happy occasion, the head of the house, the Aga, receives people of all classes at his *birooni*. Every part of the house or of the bazaar is cleaned and carpeted and decorated with fresh flowers and mirrors and other articles of beauty. In the bazaars both men and women come and go, sitting awhile on couches placed on large carpets to enjoy tea or sherbet with cookies and candies. Only men are allowed in private houses.

The sad religious occasions for public feasts are in the mourning months of Muharram, Safar, and Ramadan. Thirteen centuries ago, on the tenth of Muharram, the martyrdom of *Iman Hussein* (Mohammed's grandson) and his close relatives took place in the course of a battle with a caliph on a plain

in the southwest of Baghdad. The plain is now a city named
Karbala. This city as well as Najaf and several other cities
of Iraq near Baghdad are sacred cities for Iranians, because
Ali, the Prophet's son-in-law, and his descendants are buried
there.

For many ages the Iranians have expended enormous wealth
in those cities, building magnificent tombs and marvelous
shrines. They have presented the most precious jewelry, carpets, and valuable works of art for their adornment. Thousands
of Iranians go on pilgrimages each year to visit the shrines, and
many of the extremely faithful, when they are old, emigrate
to Karbala or Najaf to be buried near the Imam's shrine
when they die.

During the two months of Muharram and Safar people
clothe themselves in black. No marriage takes place in Iran
during these sixty days, and in many houses of wealthy men
and women mourning assemblies are arranged in the morning,
afternoon, or early evenings.

Men, women, and children gather together and sit on large,
beautiful carpets spread over the brick-paved grounds between
the pool and the flower beds. There they listen to professional
narrators who eulogize the deeds of the martyrs of Karbala.
This traditional commemoration is called *Rowze Khani*. When
the narrations are over and the people are truly affected with
grief, tea or coffee is served by men, who walk among the
seated guests offering to each a cup. Formerly, instead of tea,
they served rose water with rock candy dissolved in it—hot in
winter and icy cold in summer. In fact this is still served in
many cities. The *Rowze Khani* lasts from three to twenty days.

But the most important part of the mourning is the distribu-
tion of food to the public in the evenings of these two months.
Sofreh is the name given to these public dinners, and they are
served in the *birooni* of wealthy men or women or in the

mosques. Men of all classes, but no women, are welcome to eat of the special dishes for these occasions. Relatives of the bene-factors, neighbors, friends, priests, businessmen, and the poor, all gather together on carpets spread over the grounds. Tea is served first, then dinner. After the tea is sipped, a few pro-fessional narrators relate the tragic story of Karbala and other unhappy events in the lives of the Prophet and his relatives. People listen, shed tears of grief, and admire the bravery and unselfishness of those who sacrificed their lives as well as their possessions to establish the religion of Islam. Then dinner fol-lows, served on large wooden trays placed in front of the fol-lowers. The dinners continue from three to ten nights.

Each night a tray of foods—halva, salads, and sherbets—is sent to the houses of the various members of the family and to the home of each neighbor for the women. The exclusion of women from these ceremonies is a tradition and even now, when the women of Iran are no longer secluded from the world, they are not invited to attend. After dinner each poor man carries home to his family a large copper bowl filled with rice, chicken and meat dishes and, of course, halva.

In Ramadan another public offering of food takes place. It is traditional to feed the people at night, especially the poor, since they fast all day. Wealthy benefactors serve the very best of dishes at a feast called *Eftari*, meaning the "breaking of the fast." These ceremonies are like those of Muharram, except for special dishes, recipes for which are given farther along in the book.

During Ramadan parties and gatherings are held in the evening, because during the day the people who are eligible to fast must devote their time to praying to Allah. They relax, sleep, and pray, and set aside all the problems of material life and worldly lust. After the sun sets they are permitted to break their fast and again to enjoy living until two hours before the dawn. At that time, according to religious laws, they take the last of food, and fasting begins again.

A special dessert named "halva of milk" (*halvaye shir*) and a confection known as *zolobiya* are served at the evening parties during Ramadan. These sweets used to be made and sold only during that month, but today they are made and enjoyed at all times of the year.

OFFERINGS TO ALLAH—NAZR

Sometimes a mother desires God's protection for her child, and will make a vow to give a most valuable and delicious food or halva to the poor in order to please Allah. This is an ancient ceremony, which still takes place in Iran. Special kinds of halvas are characteristic of the different types of *Nazr* offerings.

A few days before the anticipated celebration the servants begin to prepare the particular pudding or food which is to be served. The recipients of the food are pleased, naturally, and the honored child grows up to be a happy adult, embraced in the love which prompted his parents to suffer the labor of making a *Nazr* in his behalf. A *Nazr* has an important psychological effect on a child's heart and mind.

I have never forgotten two particular holy days—the twenty-seventh of Safar and, seven months later, the last Friday of Ramadan. My mother had lost two of her children, who died before my birth. So, as an offering for my protection, she made her vow to Allah to prepare a special soup (*aashe reshte*) on one day, and a halva (*ardeh khorma*) on the other.

The whole house stirred with activity on those days. And I felt very important to be the center of so much loving attention from the older members of the family, and to be treated with respect and awe by my younger brothers and sisters and our friends. Each of my brothers and sisters, except the eldest brother, had only one *Nazr*, while the first son of the family and I had the privilege of two!

There is another *Nazr* offering which causes much amusement for the children of Persia. Once a year, when the figs are ripe, each child is weighed and the equivalent of his or her weight, in fresh red or white figs, is given to the poor. This is repeated each year until the child is about seven years old.

Large scales, with a pair of round pans hung on either end of the handle, are used. It was great fun to sit in one pan while figs were piled high in the other. One at a time we would be hoisted up into the air by a strong manservant, to be weighed. Such excitement to be swinging up there! And we always protested that we were not weighed correctly, so that the poor man would have to weigh us again and again and keep us in the air as long as his strength would permit. The figs were divided among the servants and the poor, but the weigher's portion was almost certain to be much more than that of any other.

CHAPTER II

Food and Entertainment
Within the Persian Home

Glorious is the golden disk of sun, as my Crown.
Magnificent is the celestial sphere, as my Throne,
With two loaves of bread, either made of wheat or oat,
Two pieces of clothing, either new or old,
But, with a free heart, chained with love for All,
And a freewill to help the afflicted call,
Sharing my loaves with the hungry, under the shading pines,
And rejoicing the life with friends and kin.
  Greater is such happiness
  Than the immortal life!

Sadi, the Persian poet—Twelfth century

Throughout Persia the times for serving the main meals of the day are the same everywhere, regardless of the variations in climate. Breakfast is any time from 6 A.M. to 9 A.M., depending on the preference of the family. Midday, from noon to 1 P.M., is the luncheon hour, while dinner occurs between the hours of 9 P.M. and midnight.

In addition to these main meals, everyone partakes of fruits or sherbets in midmorning, and afternoon tea is from 4 to 5 P.M.

The classic breakfast consists of hot tea and milk; bread, butter, fruit preserves, honey; white Iranian cheese, either plain or mixed with crushed walnut meats; eggs, hard, soft, or scrambled; and apples or grapes in summer—oranges or tangerines in winter. Bread, tea, and cheese are the simple breakfast of the whole nation. In the Eastern cities of Iran, during the hot, dry summers, the standard breakfast consists only of fresh fruits, and in the cold winters in other parts of the country a kind of hot cereal called *haleem* and a soup called *gipa* are enjoyed.

The midmorning refreshments in winter consist of oranges and pomegranates and, in summer, all sorts of watermelons, cantaloupes, peaches, cucumbers, romaine, and sherbets.

The foods for lunch and dinner are practically the same. One kind of *polou* or *chelou* (rice dishes) and a dish of meat (*khoresh*) is always on the table. Even if the Aga and his lady do not care for them they must, nevertheless, be made for the servants. Other kinds of meat dishes, fish, soups, desserts, yogurt, and seasonal fruits are the chief items served for both lunch and dinner.

From ancient days until the Iranians came into close contact with first the Arabs and then the Mongols, who temporarily ruled Iran, they sat on short-legged chairs, named *korsi*, and used very low tables for dining. But since those tribal rulers used no table nor chairs, but sat on the ground to eat, the Iranians gradually changed their habits. Beautifully designed, thick carpets and thick plush cushions and mattresses made the custom gracious and comfortable, and it is still, on many occasions, a delightful custom, even in houses that are furnished with the latest furniture, to sit on the floor. Of course no one would ever think of stepping into a room or over a carpet with shoes on; shoes were, and still are, removed at the entrance to such a room.

The food was placed on a clean, white cloth, or *sofreh*, which was placed over a leather *sofreh* of the same size spread on the floor. Sitting at the *sofreh*, members of the family and their guests ate everything but soup and dessert with the fingers of their right hands. For soups and desserts, a short-handled Chinese silver or wooden spoon was used.

Washing the hands carefully before each meal was adhered to strictly. I still remember vividly when the tall, slender Negro maid whose job it was to attend to the water pipe for my father, and to the hot water for washing the hands, would come into the dining room at mealtime. She had a large, shining brass bowl in one hand and a large brass jar of hot water and some towels in the other. She would kneel first in front of the guests and wash their hands, then my father's, mother's, eldest brother's, and the other children's hands followed respectively.

Although the fork and spoon are gradually replacing the fingers among all classes of Persians, you will still find these traditional eating habits and manners in vogue more or less everywhere throughout Iran.

PRIVATE PARTIES

Iranian women, secluded in the *andarooni* for many centuries, found ways and means of entertaining among themselves, and different kinds of social affairs developed. These basic social functions of Persia are still enjoyed today.

Afternoon tea parties are always popular and usually begin about four o'clock. Friends and relatives are invited to the house, but it is also usual for them to drop in on the lady of the house without a formal invitation. Cookies, candies, nuts, fruits, romaine lettuce—either with vinegar, which is often mixed with finely minced fresh chervil, or with pickles of eggplant—toasted corn, and boiled fresh lima beans are the foods most frequently served at such parties. The ladies chat, laugh, talk of serious subjects—even politics—and social affairs. In some families music is played and the guests dance and sing. Nowadays men are included in these parties, and gambling is their amusement.

All-day parties, which date 'way back into the history of the life of the Iranian women, are still carried on by the old families. The party begins at the house about 10 A.M. and continues until sunset when, in olden days, Iranian women had to be in their homes.

The guests are usually comprised of relatives and close friends from families of equal prominence. Upon the arrival of the guests, sherbets, in summer, or tea, in winter, are served. The sherbets in large glasses, the tea in smaller ones, each on a silver stand, are placed on silver trays.

About an hour later cookies, sweet breads, and fruits such as pomegranates, oranges, tangerines, apples, and pears in

winter, and other seasonal fruits in summer, are passed. Luncheon occurs between 1 and 2 P.M., and the hostess always out-
does herself to serve unusually delectable foods, halvas, and
other delicacies, arranged in the most attractive manner.

At teatime in the afternoon the same foods that were served
in the morning are again offered. At some of these all-day
parties a group of musicians would play old classical songs for
the enjoyment of the guests.

A third kind of party, and perhaps the most popular in
Persia, reflects the poetical nature of the Iranians. To visit an
informal garden in summer or a green field on a sunny day in
winter; to picnic beside the fresh, murmuring water of a brook,
where the air is filled with the fragrance of blossoms and
flowers, is to the Persians one of the most enchanting ways to
relax with friends. By sharing fine food and wine and music,
by reciting spirited and poetic anecdotes and poems in the great
outdoors, they feel and enjoy nature more deeply. These picnics, therefore, are a form of entertainment indulged in with
great frequency all over the country. Formerly they lasted until
sunset and sometimes, on a moonlit night, until early evening.
But in this modern day and age, they very often last until midnight or the following morning! Kababs and polous are the
traditional fare, served with wine.

MANNERS AND CUSTOMS
OF THE PERSIANS

Gracious hospitality is inherent in the character of the
Persian people—a characteristic as ancient and revered as history itself.

To the Persians, a guest is "a gift of God" and is, therefore, proffered the best that the host has to offer—the best food, the most comfortable chair. The host never sits at the head of the table, but stays in the background, and it is not unfrequent for him to go hungry, so engrossed is he in attending the needs and pleasures of his guests. Even if the guest should be an enemy, no discourtesy is ever dreamed of.

When a visitor is present in the home, no host sits while his guest is standing, nor does he ever turn his back or speak harshly. As a matter of fact, in the code of Iranian good manners such actions on either side are considered insulting.

There are stories in the history of Iran concerning defeated warriors who, by simply going to the house of their conquerors, were generously and graciously received.

An old folk tale illustrates the emphasis put on the host-guest relationship: One night a king, who had lost his way while hunting, reached the small tent of an old women who lived far out on the lonely plains. Her only source of food was the milk of the goat she possessed.

The king asked her if he could stay for the night and was cheerfully welcomed by the old woman, who never suspected she was entertaining royalty. For dinner he was served an especially delicious kabab of fresh meat. The next morning, as the king was preparing to depart, he asked:

"Where did you get fresh meat in such a deserted place as this?"

"I had a goat, brother," she humbly replied.

"Ah, your only source of life," he asked in amazement, "and you killed it to feed me?"

"Source or no source," she said, "I could not let my guest sleep hungry." And she smiled.

Then the king asked her to go with him to his palace, where she was blessed with many kindnesses.

CHAPTER III

The Fundamentals of Classic Persian Cooking

When the Sultan Shah-Zaman
Goes to the city Ispahan
Even before he gets so far
As the place where the clustered palm-trees are,
At the last of the thirty palace-gates,
The pet of the haram, Rose-Bloom
Orders a feast in his favorite room—
Glittering square of colored ice,
Sweetened with syrup, tinctured with spice,
Creams and cordials, and sugared dates,
Syrian apples, Othmanee quinces
Limes and citrons and apricots
And wines that are known to Eastern princes.

      T. B. Aldrich—"When the Sultan Goes to Ispahan."

Most of the ingredients used in Persian cooking are available in the United States today. Rice flour, puffed peas, saffron, and Iranian cheeses can be found in Italian, Armenian, and Greek markets. The fresh vegetables, the dry vegetables, seeds, and spices used in Persian foods are at hand in most of the chain stores in America. And the necessary kitchen equipment can be found in almost every home.

The techniques for preparing the ingredients listed here briefly are the basic principles of Persian cooking. And the methods for preparing halva, sweets, and sherbets are described in the recipes in the latter part of this book.

UTENSILS

Of first importance in Persian cooking are the pots, pans, skillets, and saucepans, and the materials of which they are made. The shapes of some of these utensils often differ from the shapes of those used in America, especially those used for the cooking of rice. But substitutes can easily be made.

All vessels—caldrons, spatulas, ladles, colanders, et cetera—are made only of copper, but are always lined or coated with tin. The tin is renewed as soon as it begins to wear off. Recently aluminum pans have come into use in Persia, but nothing is ever cooked in an iron vessel. But no matter what metal the utensil is made of—brass, copper, aluminum, or enamel—it is most essential that the vessels be thick and heavy-bottomed.

The Persian saucepan for cooking rice is called *deeg*, and it has a special shape, patterned from ancient times. It is deep, with a narrow top and a wide bottom. The saucepan used for making halva, sherbets, and other sweetmeats has a wide-open top and a round, small bottom. The strainer for rinsing rice should be large and shallow.

BASIC INGREDIENTS

Oil

The best kind of fat for any Persian food is clarified butter. A second choice is vegetable oil, but in America I have used chicken fat and margarine for all kinds of rice dishes, and vegetable oils for pastries, and found them satisfactory. No pork fat is ever used in Persia.

Rice

To make a fluffy rice, the rice should be very hard, yellowish in color with no broken grains, and at least two years old. The harder the rice grains, the more feathery the rice dish will be. There are many varieties of Persian rice, all superb in quality. If you can obtain Persian rice do so, otherwise be sure to buy fine-quality, long-grained rice.

Meat

The Iranians prefer mutton and lamb to beef. Beef is very cheap and is regarded as second-grade meat. It is used chiefly by the third class of people and the villagers. Meats in order of preference are: fowl, venison, lamb, mutton, and veal. Pork and pork products are not common food for the nation. It is used by a small minority of Christians, foreigners, and some of the younger generation familiar with European customs.

Rice Flour

From ancient times many puddings and sweetmeats in Persia have been made with rice flour, which you can buy in any market. But in America it can be found only in fine bakeries and, sometimes, in the health-food stores of large cities. However, it is easily prepared at home as follows:

Wash rice of any kind, three or four times. Then spread it to dry. While still damp, pound it in a deep mortar with a heavy pestle or pass it through a fine grinder. Powder it fine by pounding and sifting alternately until all the rice is converted into a very soft white powder. Spread the powder to dry thoroughly. Placing it in a very warm oven will speed the process. Store in a tightly stoppered glass jar in a cool, dry place.

If you own an electric blender, simply measure ½ cup raw rice into the container, cover, and blend at high speed for about two minutes, or until the rice is reduced to a fine powder.

Verjuice

This is the sour juice of unripe, green grapes which is used in all parts of Persia in soups and meat dishes. It is also considered by Persian physicians as an important medicine for liver disturbances and as a relief from rheumatism. When late spring arrives and the grapes are still green, part of them are sent to the markets, where homemakers whose job it is to bottle the juice for sale in shops buy what they need. The juice is very sour indeed—much more so than the juice of lemons or limes. But lime juice may be substituted for it in recipes.

Puffed Peas, or Nokhodchi

Peas processed in a way that puffs them and makes them edible, with the flavor of a nut, are used extensively in Persian cooking. They are available at most Italian or Greek stores for a reasonable price. (Italians call them *chichi*.) Flour made from these peas in the same way that rice flour is made from rice is used in puddings and cookies.

Ajeel

This is a combination of puffed peas, shelled pistachios, almonds, hazelnuts, pumpkin and watermelon seeds cooked in salted water and then roasted. It is served with drinks at Persian parties. Homemade *ajeel* is cooked in half salted water and half lime juice before being roasted.

Dried Limes, or Limu Omani

Fresh limes are boiled in slightly salted water for five minutes and left to dry in the sunshine. When dry, they are stored in tightly closed boxes and used in soups and meat dishes, to which they add a delicious and unusual flavor.

Spices

In general Persian foods are only mildly spiced in contrast to the highly spiced curries of India and Indonesia. Saffron and turmeric are the most popular seasonings, and both are always finely powdered for use.

From earliest times saffron, because of its delicate flavor and perfume, has been used to flavor rice and meat dishes as well as puddings, halvas, and other sweets. Saffron is made from the stamens of small yellow flowers which grow abundantly in different parts of Persia. The flowers are collected, dried, and sold in the markets. Persian saffron is an important item of export. It must be kept tightly stoppered in a glass or china container. When used, a pinch of saffron is pounded in a small mortar until it turns to a fine powder. After it is ground, a few drops of hot water are added to form a thick, pungent liquid. If dry saffron is added to hot oil, it will lose color and will not impart its flavor to the food. So always mix it first with a little hot water, then add it to the hot oil for polous.

Turmeric is used especially in meat dishes. Like curry powder, it is generally cooked in a little oil with onion and black pepper before it is added to the other ingredients.

All kinds of peppers and hot spices are also used in Persian cooking, but always in limited quantities, for the food of Persia is delicate, gently seasoned; some of the dishes are fragrant with the more aromatic spices such as cardamom, cinnamon, and clove.

Tangerine Shreds, or Khelale Narangi

Tangerine peel plays a large role in flavoring Persian foods. The white, bitter layer beneath the skin is carefully removed with a sharp knife, and the yellow peel is cut into very fine shreds about one inch in length. These shreds are then dried and stored in a tightly covered glass jar for future use. When it is used, as much as is needed is put into cold water and boiled for about five minutes. It is then rinsed, covered with fresh water, and boiled again for two minutes. A final rinsing removes any bitterness, and the shreds are ready for use.

Essences of Flowers

The distillations of flower petals and blossoms are used in various foods—sweets, puddings, and beverages. For many centuries rose and orange flower water have been employed not only as perfume, but as ingredients in cooking.

In Persia there grows a special kind of rose which is small and pink—a sort of wild rose—but it has such a strong scent that one small bud will perfume an entire room. This is the rose that is used for distillation, and the pure scent is extracted and exported to many parts of the world. The name of this rose is Damask, but in Persia it is simply called the Red Rose.

The Red Rose is symbolic of the color and fragrance of a beautiful girl, and in Persian poetry a beloved is often called *Gole,* meaning the Red Rose.

In Persian literature, the nightingale is everlastingly frenzied with love for this rose, and the whole night long he sings only the enchanting songs of love for his *Gole.*

Small white roses, orange and quince blossoms, pussy willows, the peels of citrus fruits and the seeds of the anise and fennel are also distilled for use in cooking.

Herbs

History reveals that the Persians were one of the first peoples to use many varieties of herbs as parts of food, either for the sake of their flavors or for their medicinal benefits. Most of these herbs and flavorful plants grow in America, but Americans do not seem to know how to use them or realize the extent to which their flavor can improve a dish.

One particular leaf, common in America, which appears in many Persian recipes, is mint. The leaves are picked from the stalk, dried, and kept in a tightly closed box or jar. As needed, the leaves are finely powdered before use.

Another delicious green plant, popular in Persian cooking, grows abundantly in the spring in the mountainous regions of Persia. It is a kind of cardoon, called *kangar.* It is thistlelike, related to the artichoke family, with a soft, small, edible stalk and a tender heart. But it is full of prickles and must be handled with care. I have not found this vegetable growing in California, but I am sure it grows elsewhere in the United States. In Persia it is cooked and combined with rice or meat, or served with yogurt as a salad with kababs.

In the farms throughout the country it is cooked, combined with yogurt, and stored in a goatskin. This is called *kangar mast,* and after remaining in the skin for a week or two it is particularly delicious.

I will always remember the thrill, as a child, when with my brothers and sisters I waited impatiently for winter to end, because each year with the coming of spring our farmers would bring the large goatskins filled with *kangar mast* from the village. Some of it my mother would send to relatives and friends as gifts; some she would give to the servants to take home, but a good share was kept in the supply room for us. At any time we children wished we were allowed to eat all we wanted of it, regardless of whether it was just before mealtime or not.

In later years I tried making it myself and modernized the procedure by keeping it in a china bowl. The result was good, but still it was not the same as that brought from the village in the goatskin!

Bos-hac, in his *Divan* has a satirical anecdote about the *kangar.*

"As a token of gratitude to the camel who has never hurt the earth by his soft feet, the Earth grows prickles which the camel, because of his extremely affable nature, leaves as a blessed gift for our lips and teeth. And we, sons of Adam, cook it, mix it with yogurt and serve it with kababs. Therefore, it seems that the taste of the camel and that of Man are alike."

In Persia the camel is symbolic of stupidity and lack of common sense, intelligence, and talent!

Part Two

The Classic Cuisine
of Persia

✐ Chelou and Polou

(Persian-Style Rice)

Perhaps *polou* is the most traditional dish in all of Persia, and certainly rice, which forms the basis of both *polou* and *chelou*, is the most important food commodity in Persian cuisine. The method of cooking both *polou* and *chelou* produces delicate dishes which are different in taste and texture from any of the well-known Chinese, Arabic, or Spanish rice dishes. The rice is delicately perfumed, each grain white, feathery, and fluffy and apart from any other. It is essential that the rice be cooked in plenty of water. As a general rule, one pound of rice should be covered with hot water to a depth of 8 to 10 inches.

CHELOU

(Serves 3)

Chelou is simply cooked, buttered rice which is baked in the oven in such a way as to form a crunchy crust in the bottom of the pan. This crust I fondly call the crispy-crunchy.

Chelou is always served with meat dishes having a thick sauce, called *khoreshes* (see Index).

Wash thoroughly one pound long-grained rice. Fill a 4-quart saucepan with water and bring to a boil. When boiling steadily, add the rice and 3 tablespoons salt and boil, uncovered, for 7 to 10 minutes over high heat. Stir the water occasionally, being careful not to break the rice grains. Be careful, also, not to over-cook the rice. It is done when it is cooked at the core. Test a grain by biting it in half. Remove immediately from heat, drain in a colander, and rinse with lukewarm water to remove excess starch. The larger the pan used to boil the rice, the more feathery the grains will be. If the rice is tasteless after being rinsed, bathe it again with about 1 pint strong, lukewarm salt water.

Heat a heavy-bottomed saucepan or flameproof casserole over a low flame and add 2 tablespoons cooking oil or melted butter mixed with 1 tablespoon hot water. Swirl pan to coat it evenly with the mixture. Mix ½ cup cooked rice with 1 egg yolk, slightly beaten, and spread it evenly over the bottom of the pan. Fill the pan with the remaining cooked rice, mounding it up in the center. With the handle of a long-handled spoon make a deep hole in the center of the mound, cover, and bake in a 350° oven for 15 minutes. Remove cover and sprinkle rice with 2 or 3 tablespoons hot butter or any good oil mixed with 2 tablespoons hot water. Cover and bake for 30 minutes longer. Remove from oven and place pan, covered, on a cool surface for 10 minutes. This makes it easier to remove the brown crust in the bottom of the pan. Uncover pan and stir rice gently with a spatula to make it fluffy. Turn rice out onto a warm serving dish in a mound. Then remove the brown crust and serve it separately, or heap it over the rice on the serving platter.

NOTE: Instead of mixing the rice with egg yolk to form the crust, you may use ¼ cup milk or 3 tablespoons yogurt, or 1 medium fresh tomato, peeled and chopped.

POLOUS—CLASSICAL AND SIMPLE

And nearer as they came, a genial savour
Of certain stews, and roasts-meats, and Pilaus,
Things which in hungry mortals' eyes find favour.

Byron—Don Juan. *Canto V, St. 47*

When rice, cooked and drained, is mixed with any kind of vegetable, fruit, fowl, meat, or nuts, it is called *polou*. A generous amount of butter is used to coat the rice, and saffron, chopped almonds, pistachios, or spices are usually used for flavoring. If chicken for *polou* is small, it may be sautéed and placed in the center of the *polou*. If large, it is better to boil it with a little water and 1 medium onion until tender, then place it in the center of the rice. The broth then should be mixed with the butter in place of hot water, and poured over the rice.

SWEET POLOU
(*Shecar Polou*)

This ancient *polou*, served with its accompanying minced-meat dish (*Qa'meh khoresh*), has always been mandatory at weddings, other important celebrations, and religious public feedings. It is a great favorite with the Persians. In olden days it was called *moza'far* (meaning yellow with saffron), or yellow rice.

    1 cup sugar
    ½ cup water
    3 ounces shredded dried tangerine peel
    1 medium onion
    ½ pound ground lean veal or beef
    1 teaspoon salt
    ½ teaspoon black pepper
    ½ teaspoon turmeric
    A pinch of clove (if desired)
    1 pound long-grained rice
    Butter or oil
    ½ teaspoon saffron
    ⅔ cup melted butter or chicken fat
    ½ cup finely chopped blanched almonds
    ½ cup chopped pistachios   (Serves 3)

In a heavy-bottomed saucepan combine sugar and water. Boil rapidly to a thick syrup, or until syrup spins a long thread. Prepare tangerine peel (see Index), add it to the boiling syrup, and boil for 3 minutes longer.

Grind the onion and mix it with the meat. Season with salt, pepper, turmeric, and clove. Form the meat into small balls the size of hazelnuts and sauté in a little butter or oil until brown on all sides.

Cook rice according to directions for cooking *chelou* and drain thoroughly. Mix the syrup and meat balls with the rice, stirring the rice slowly and carefully so that each grain is coated with the syrup. Oil the inside of a deep casserole and put in the rice mixture, mounding it up in the center. Bake in a preheated 350° oven for 45 minutes and continue as for *chelou*. Then place rice on a large serving dish.

Grind saffron to a powder and mix with a little hot water

to form a thick paste. Combine paste with the hot melted butter or chicken fat and pour over the rice. Stir and mix gently until all the grains, especially those on top, become yellow with the saffron. Sprinkle with the almonds and pistachios.

NOTE: Chicken may be used in place of the meat balls. Sauté the chicken in a little butter or oil until brown on all sides and place it in the center of the rice before it is baked. To serve: Place chicken in center of the serving platter and surround by the saffron rice. When this *polou* is served with *Qa'meh*, chicken or meat balls are not generally used.

CLASSICAL CHERRY POLOU

Sweet *polous* such as this exotic cherry polou are served either with tiny meat balls, as in the following recipe, or with *Qa'meh khoresh* (see Index). If *Qa'meh* is served, the meat balls are omitted.

 2½ pounds long-grained rice
 1 cup sugar
 2½ pounds pitted fresh sour cherries
 1 pound ground meat
 1 onion, finely chopped
 ½ cup butter or margarine
 Salt and pepper to taste
 5 ounces (½ cup) blanched chopped almonds or pistachios
 ½ teaspoon saffron

(Serves 4)

Cook rice according to directions for *chelou* and drain. Mix sugar and cherries, bring to a boil, and boil until syrup is thick. Combine meat and onion, season, and form into small meat balls. Sauté the meat balls in the butter until browned on all sides; mix with the cherries and rice and season to taste with salt. Oil the inside of a heavy saucepan or flameproof deep casserole as follows: put in the pan 2 tablespoons oil or melted butter mixed with 1 tablespoon hot water and swirl pan to coat it with the mixture. Place pan over low heat and fill with the rice-cherries-meat mixture, mounding it up in the center. With the handle of a long-handled spoon make a deep hole in the center of the mound, cover, and bake in a preheated 350° oven for 45 minutes. Uncover pan and stir rice gently with a spatula or large spoon. Turn out on a serving dish in a mound and sprinkle with the chopped nuts and saffron prepared with 2 tablespoons oil.

CLASSICAL TURKEY POLOU

This *polou* is prepared chiefly for large parties and receptions. It is frequently served for wedding dinners or the celebration dinner of the birth of a baby.

    2 pounds long-grained rice
    1 small turkey
    1 large onion, chopped
    1 cup butter or cooking oil
    2 cups hot water
    ½ pound mixed dried prunes, plums, barberries, and
        apricots
    Salt and pepper to taste
    ⅓ teaspoon cloves
    ¾ cup hot turkey broth
    ¼ pound currants
    3 tablespoons cuminseed
    1 teaspoon saffron   (Serves 8)

Cook rice according to directions for *chelou* and drain. Wash inside of turkey thoroughly and make four or five incisions with a sharp knife on different parts of the breast. Sauté the turkey slightly with the onion in ½ cup of the butter in a large deep pot until browned on all sides. Add the water, cover closely, and simmer over very low heat about 3 hours, or until turkey is tender. Then uncover and cook until browned on all sides. Remove, stuff the inside with the mixed dried fruits, and sprinkle generously with salt, pepper, and cloves. Coat the inside of a large saucepan with ¼ cup butter mixed with ½ cup of the turkey broth. Place the pan over low heat and pour in half the rice. Place turkey in center and sprinkle with fried currants and cuminseeds. Cover with remainder of the rice. Make a hole in the center of the rice, cover, and bake in a preheated 350° oven for 20 minutes. Remove pan, sprinkle with remaining butter mixed with remaining broth, cover, and bake again for 30 minutes longer. To serve, place turkey on a large serving platter. Moisten the saffron with a little hot broth and add it to the rice, carefully stirring the rice with a spatula to mix it well with the currants and seeds. Surround the turkey with the rice. This *polou* is served with *Qa'meh* and pickles.

CLASSICAL TOMATO POLOU

1 pound lean ground beef
Salt and pepper to taste
½ cup butter or oil
1 large onion, finely chopped
½ teaspoon curry or clove
1 pound long-grained rice, washed and drained
4 cups tomato juice

(Serves 2 to 3)

Season the meat with salt and pepper and form it into tiny balls the size of hazelnuts. Sauté the meat balls in a deep casserole in 2 tablespoons of the butter or oil until brown on all sides. Remove meat and sauté the onion and curry in the oil remaining in the pan. When onion is lightly browned, add the rice and the remaining butter or oil and sauté until the rice is brown. Add tomato juice and enough water to completely cover the rice by about 1 inch. Cover the top of the pot with a thick towel, then cover closely with the lid. Simmer over very low heat for about 35 minutes, or until the water is completely absorbed by the rice. Mix the meat balls with the rice. Make a hole in the center. Cover and bake in a preheated 350° oven for 45 minutes. Serve hot with sour pickles.

NOTE: If chicken is preferred to meat, sauté the chicken until brown on all sides, then steam with a little water or broth until tender. Place the chicken in the center of the rice and bake as usual. One small eggplant, peeled, chopped, and fried, or 1 cup cooked string beans or peas may be added to the rice. Chicken may be substituted for the meat balls.

TOMATO AND EGGPLANT POLOU

1 pound long-grained rice
4 cups tomato juice
½ pound ground meat
1 small onion, grated
½ teaspoon salt
¼ teaspoon pepper
½ teaspoon turmeric
6 tablespoons butter
1 very small eggplant, peeled and chopped
4 tablespoons cooking oil
1 tablespoon hot water
1 egg
½ tablespoon saffron   (Serves 3 to 4)

Wash rice thoroughly. Put it in a large saucepan and add enough water to cover the rice by a depth of one inch. Cover top with a towel, then with the lid, and simmer over very low heat for 30 minutes, or until there is only a little water left. Add tomato juice, stir well, cover, and simmer over low heat for another 20 minutes, or until all the moisture has been absorbed. Combine meat, grated onion, salt, pepper, and turmeric, form into small balls and sauté in 2 tablespoons of the butter until brown on all sides. Remove balls, add 4 tablespoons butter and fry the eggplant until soft.

Coat a large deep casserole with 2 tablespoons of the oil mixed with the hot water. Beat the egg well and mix 2 tablespoons of the rice and sprinkle over bottom of pan. Add half the rice, then the meat balls and eggplant, and cover with remainder of the rice, mounding it up and forming a hole in the center. Cover and bake in a preheated 350° oven for 45 minutes.

To serve: place the casserole over a basin of cold water for 10 to 15 minutes, then remove contents in one piece, like a large ball. Mix saffron with a little hot water and add to remaining oil, heated. Pour over the mound of rice.

EASY TOMATO POLOU

2 pounds long-grained rice
1 pound boneless shoulder of lamb or veal
1 onion, chopped
½ cup butter or margarine
4 cups tomato juice
Salt and pepper
3 eggs, lightly beaten
2 tablespoons oil
1 tablespoon hot water   (Serves 6)

Cook the rice according to the recipe for *chelou*, but not so soft. Rinse and drain. Cook the meat with the onion in water to cover. Add butter, tomato juice, and salt and pepper to taste. Cover and boil until the tomato juice is reduced to a thick gravy. Coat the inside of a deep casserole with the oil mixed with the hot water. Put half the rice in the bottom. Put first the meat and then half the gravy over the rice and pour over the eggs. Now cover with remaining rice and pour the remaining gravy over the rice. Make into a mound with a hole in the center. Cover and bake in a preheated 350° oven for 45 minutes. Serve hot with pickles.

CLASSICAL YOGURT POLOU
(Tah Chin)

This is a "party" *polou,* also served for very special guests.

    3 cups yogurt
    Salt and pepper to taste
    1 teaspoon saffron
    1 pound lamb or veal shank or round
    1½ pounds long-grained rice
    2 eggs
    6 tablespoons melted butter, or any good oil

(Serves 4)

Season 1½ cups of the yogurt with salt, pepper, and ½ teaspoon of the saffron. Cut the meat into large cubes and soak it in the seasoned yogurt for 5 to 10 hours. Then cook the rice according to the directions for cooking *chelou,* but cook it for 5 minutes only. It must not be soft. Rinse rice and drain. Beat the eggs and mix with ½ cup of the yogurt and 1 cup cooked rice. Coat the inside of a deep casserole with melted butter mixed with 1 tablespoon hot water and put the rice-yogurt mixture in the bottom for a crusty layer. Put a layer of meat over this and add 2 to 3 tablespoons yogurt in which meat was soaked. Then add a cup of rice. Repeat the layers of meat, yogurt, and rice, ending with rice, and pour any remaining yogurt over the top. Make a hole in the center, cover, and bake in a preheated 350° oven for 45 minutes.

To serve, spoon the soft rice and meat onto a serving platter and place the crispy-crunchy layer on top. Sprinkle with the remaining saffron mixed with a little water and melted butter or oil. Serve hot and with no pickle.

NOTE: If desired, ½ pound fresh spinach may be washed, chopped, drained, and fried in 1 tablespoon butter. Add the spinach to the meat and yogurt mixture and, when making the layers, put some of the spinach over the meat, then the yogurt, and then the rice.

CLASSICAL CARROT POLOU

½ pound ground lamb or veal
1 onion, grated
½ teaspoon turmeric
½ teaspoon pepper
1 teaspoon salt
½ cup butter or any good cooking oil
1½ pounds fresh carrots, grated
½ cup lemon juice
3 tablespoons sugar
1 pound long-grained rice
1 teaspoon saffron
1 tablespoon hot water
4 tablespoons cooking oil or melted butter

(Serves 3 to 4)

Mix meat with the onion, turmeric, pepper, and salt. Make tiny balls of the meat and sauté them in the butter or oil until browned on all sides. Remove the meat, add the grated carrots, and continue to sauté until the carrots are lightly browned. Add lemon juice and sugar, cover, and cook over low heat until the carrots are soft and the gravy is thick.

Cook rice according to the directions for *chelou*, rinse, and drain. Mix the rice with the carrots and gravy, put it into an oiled deep casserole and bake in a preheated 350° oven for 45 minutes. Mix saffron with the hot water and cooking oil or melted butter and stir lightly into the rice. Serve hot with *Qa'meh* and any kind of pickles.

EASY LENTIL POLOU
(*Adas Polou*)

¾ pound lentils
1 pound long-grained rice
2 tablespoons cooking oil
1 tablespoon hot water
1 pound diced cooked lamb, veal, or chicken
¼ pound stoned dates
¼ pound currants
½ teaspoon saffron
½ cup melted butter or margarine

(Serves 3 to 4)

Wash lentils, cover with lightly salted water, and cook until tender. Drain. Cook the rice according to the directions for *chelou* and mix with the cooked lentils. Coat inside of a deep casserole with the 2 tablespoons oil mixed with the hot water. Place casserole over low heat and pour in half the rice and lentils. Place meat on top and sprinkle with the dates and currants. Add remaining rice, mounding it up, and make a hole in the center. Cover and bake in a preheated 350° oven for 45 minutes. Just before serving, mix saffron with a little hot water and with the ½ cup melted butter or margarine and stir lightly into the *polou*.

NOTE: If desired, 2 or 3 whole hard-cooked eggs may be added with the meat. This *polou* may also be served with *Qa'meh* instead of with meat or chicken. In this case just use dates, currants, and eggs for the filling. Serve hot with pickles.

EASY CHICKEN POLOU
(*Morgh Polou*)

This is the chicken *polou* generally served at the Persian New Year in the southern region of Persia, with the chicken placed on the *haft seen* table (the "table of the seven S's"). The amount of rice and number of chickens needed depend upon the size of the family or the number of guests. The following quantities are designed to serve 5.

    2 pounds long-grained rice
    1 large chicken
    ¼ pound currants
    2 ounces cuminseeds
    ½ cup (1 stick) butter or any good cooking oil
    1 teaspoon saffron

This *polou* is made in exactly the same way as the turkey *polou* on page 64. The chicken is sautéed and steamed, but it is not stuffed. Serve hot with *Qa'meh* and pickles.

VEGETABLE POLOU
(Sabzi Polou)

In the north of Persia the Nowrooze *polou* is served with
the fish and vegetables placed on the *haft seen* table, instead
of the chicken.

    2 pounds long-grained rice
    1½ pounds of equal parts of fresh spinach, dill, green
        onion tops, coriander (if available), and fresh
        parsley
    6 pieces white fish fillets
    ¼ cup shortening or good cooking oil
    1 teaspoon saffron
    1 tablespoon hot water
    3 tablespoons cooking oil

(Serves 6)

Prepare the rice according to directions for *chelou* and
drain. Wash the greens, chop fine, and cook in the water
adhering to the leaves until wilted. Mix greens with the rice.
Sauté the fish in the ¼ cup shortening until lightly browned
on both sides. Put half the rice in an oiled deep saucepan or
casserole. Arrange pieces of fish over the rice and cover with
remaining rice. Make a hole in the center, cover the pot
tightly, and bake in a preheated 350° oven for 1 hour. Just
before serving, mix saffron with the water and the 3 tablespoons oil and sprinkle over the rice.

NOTE: If desired, you may omit the vegetables, mix the rice
with 3 ounces cuminseeds, ½ teaspoon saffron, and ¼ pound
currants and serve with fried fish. This is called fish polou or
mahi polou. Either kind of fish polou is served with *Qa'meh*
and eggplant, or pickles.

LIMA BEAN and DILL POLOU
(Sheved Bagla)

1½ pounds long-grained rice
1½ pounds fresh dill
1 box frozen lima beans, cooked and drained
1 pound boneless lamb or veal from shoulder, shank, or
    round
Salt and pepper to taste
1 large onion
½ teaspoon turmeric
3 tablespoons cooking oil
½ cup any good oil or butter
½ teaspoon saffron
1 tablespoon hot water

(Serves 3 to 4)

Cook rice according to directions for cooking *chelou* and drain. Mince the dill very fine and mix with the lima beans and rice. Stew the meat in one piece, with salt and pepper to taste, the onion, turmeric, and a little water for 2 hours, or until very tender. Then oil the inside of a large saucepan or casserole with the 3 tablespoons oil and put in half the rice. Place the meat in the center of the rice, cover with remaining rice, and make a hole in the center. Cover casserole and bake in a preheated 350° oven for 20 minutes. Then mix half the butter or oil with ¼ cup of the broth in which the meat was cooked, pour over the rice, cover, and continue to bake for 35 minutes longer. Place pot on a cool surface for 10 minutes, then turn out rice onto a large, hot serving platter. Mix saffron with the hot water and the remaining oil or butter and sprinkle over the rice. Stir rice gently with a spatula to coat the grains with the yellow saffron. Place the meat in a separate dish and the crispy-crunchy, or bottom crust, in another. Serve with

Qa'meh and any pickle or yogurt, and serve buttermilk for a beverage. But yogurt mixed with water, salt, pepper, and powdered mint leaves, called *doogh* (see Index) is best with this *polou*.

NOTE: A chicken may be substituted for the meat.

LAMB POLOU
(Barreh Polou)

This is a very popular *polou* which is served at both formal and informal receptions, private parties, and dinners as well as luncheons given in honor of one or more special guests. Boshac speaks highly of it.

> O thou! with Lamb-Pilou and Halva, and I with Date-Lentill
> He who granted that regal dish to the kings
> Gave also this humble dish to the poor!

Braise half a baby lamb or a saddle of spring lamb in a large deep pan with ½ teaspoon pepper, ½ teaspoon turmeric, 1 large onion, chopped, and 1 cup water. When well done, sprinkle with salt and place in the center of a large casserole of rice as for *chelou*. Bake in a preheated 350° oven for 45 minutes and sprinkle the rice generously with melted butter or oil. Prepare saffron (see Index), fried caraway seeds, and currants and mix well with rice. The amount of rice for this *polou* depends on the number of guests. When serving, place the meat in the center of the rice on a large warm serving dish. Serve with pickles and *Qa'meh*.

KATEH POLOU

This *polou* belongs to northern Persia. The people of Rasht, a large city on the shores of the Caspian Sea, are famous for it. It doesn't need any oil or butter and is made in the shape of a cake. It is served cold with any kind of *khoresh* and pickles, and is a perfect dish for hot summer days.

Cook 1 pound rice according to directions for cooking *chelou*, only increase the cooking time by about 15 minutes, until rice is very soft. Rinse only once and put it into an oiled casserole. Bake, tightly covered, in a preheated 350° oven for 45 minutes, without taking it out to sprinkle with butter as in other *polous*. Remove pan from oven and uncover. Let cool for 10 minutes, then spread a very white cotton cloth over the rice, still in the pan. Press it hard against the bottom and sides with the palms of the hands to crush the rice kernels together to form a cake. Place casserole over a bowl of cold water for ½ hour to cool. Then cut into squares or oblongs and arrange the pieces upside down on a serving dish, with the brown, crispy layer on top.

Dami

This is a kind of quick *chelou* which is not rinsed or drained. It is richer than the average *chelou* and very easy to make. When *dami* is served with any kind of *khoresh*, it is made plain, otherwise it is mixed with many other ingredients such as those used in *polous*.

PLAIN DAMI

Wash 1 pound long-grained rice thoroughly in cold water. Put into a deep saucepan and add enough water to cover the

rice by about 1 inch. Add 1 teaspoon salt and 3 tablespoons
butter or oil. Cover tightly, first with a towel and then with a
lid, and simmer over a very low heat about 30 minutes, or until
all the water is gone. Check it once to see if the water has
boiled away. Check a kernel with the teeth, and if still rather
hard, add half a cup of hot water by sprinkling it over and
around the rice, stir gently, cover again, and simmer for a few
minutes longer. Then take off the cloth, add 4 tablespoons of
melted butter or oil, cover again, this time only with the lid of
the pan, and bake in a preheated 350° oven for 20 to 30 minutes. Remove and serve like other *chelous* with *khoresh* and
pickles.

CURRANT DAMI

(Serves 3 to 4)

Sauté ½ onion, finely chopped, 3 ounces crushed walnuts,
and ½ pound currants in a little butter until onion is transparent. Stir in ½ teaspoon clove, nutmeg, or curry powder.
Steam rice in the same way as for plain *dami*. When all the
water has boiled away, place the currant-nut mixture in center
of rice in same casserole. Cover with rice and bake, covered, in
a preheated 350° oven for 20 minutes. Remove, mix all
together, and sprinkle with prepared saffron (see Index) and
melted butter or oil. Serve with *Qa'meh* and any kind of pickle.

SOUR-CHERRY DAMI

Pit 10 ounces of sour black cherries. Grind ½ pound meat
and make into tiny meat balls, or simply cut ½ pound meat
into small pieces. Sauté the meat with half an onion, finely

grated, in a little butter until meat is browned. Add ½ pound chopped walnuts, 2 ounces currants, the cherries, and 2 ounces chopped dried apricots. Mix all together with the well-washed rice. Add water to cover the rice by one inch. Cover with a towel and a lid and proceed as for other *dami*.

Abgushtes

(*Soups*)

How dignified looks Abgusht
With a mantle of bread on his shoulder,
And a necklace of peas around his neck!"

There are many ancient, classic soups in Persian cuisine. Although inexpensive to make, and a favorite of all classes, both rich and poor, they are looked upon as humble food. Made of meats, vegetables, legumes, and fruits, soups frequently make a meal in themselves, or precede a *polou* at the luncheon table. They are served with chopped fresh herbs, radishes, chopped onion, fresh mint leaves, bread, and pickles. Being modest in manner, the Persians, when inviting their friends to lunch or dinner, use as expression of modesty meaning, "Please give me the pleasure of taking a humble morsel of my soup and bread."

LENTIL SOUP
(*Abgushte Adas*)

1 pound brisket of lamb or veal
2 cups lentils
1 large onion, chopped
½ teaspoon each turmeric and pepper
3 to 4 dried limes
2 cups hot water
½ small head cabbage, chopped
1 teaspoon salt

(Serves 6)

Put meat and lentils into a deep saucepan and add onion, spices, limes, and hot water. Cover tightly and stew over low heat for 1 hour. Add cabbage and salt. Cover and simmer again for another hour, or until meat is very tender. Strain off liquid to serve separately. Remove bones and pound remaining ingredients in the pan with a heavy wooden pestle or potato masher. Shape into a mound in a serving dish and decorate with sliced onions. Red beans may be used instead of lentils, in which case cabbage is not used. Serve hot or cold with bread, pickles, herbs, and radishes.

POUNDED MEAT SOUP
(Gushte Kubideh)

This favorite dish is frequently served at picnics and as a snack with beverages. It is spread on bread and served with white and red radishes, fresh onion and herbs, pickles or cucumber borani (see Index).

1 pound brisket of lamb or veal
1 cup yellow split peas
½ cup large, dried white beans
¼ small green pepper, chopped
1 large potato, peeled and diced
2 large tomatoes, peeled and quartered
1 large onion, chopped
½ teaspoon each turmeric and pepper
1 teaspoon salt
2 cups hot water   (Serves 4)

Trim and wipe meat. Put all ingredients into a deep saucepan, cover tightly, and simmer over low heat about 1 hour. Uncover and continue cooking, stirring vigorously, until liquid is partially cooked away. Strain off soup to serve separately. Then pound the remaining mixture with a heavy wooden pestle or potato masher until blended to a paste, removing any bones and skin. Put the mixture into a serving dish, forming it into a mound, and decorate with sliced red and white onions and red radishes. It is ready for sandwiches or for snacks and can be served hot or cold. If decorated and kept in the refrigerator for several days, the onion flavor will permeate the meat, and if a small peeled eggplant is cooked with the other ingredients, it makes the dish even more delicious.

QUINCE SOUP
(*Abgushte Beh*)

1 pound brisket or shank of lamb or veal
1 large onion, chopped
3 ounces red beans or split peas
3 cups hot water
½ teaspoon each turmeric, pepper, and clove
1 teaspoon salt
1 large quince
1 tablespoon cooking oil
½ cup lemon or pomegranate juice
Brown sugar to taste

(Serves 4)

Put meat, onion, beans, water, and seasonings into a saucepan, cover tightly, and simmer over low heat about 1 hour. Peel and chop the quince and sauté it lightly in the oil, until partially cooked. Add to the soup along with the fruit juice. Stir in sugar to taste. Cover tightly and simmer about 1 hour longer. Strain soup, discard bones, and pound the meat. Form the meat into a mound in a serving dish, decorate with sliced onions and radishes, and serve with bread, pickles, and herbs. Serve soup separately.

DRIED-FRUIT SOUP
(*Abgushte Miveh*)

1 pound shank of lamb or veal
½ cup mixed dried red beans and yellow split peas
1 small fresh beet
1 onion, chopped
½ tablespoon turmeric, pepper, curry or clove or saffron
1 teaspoon salt
3 cups hot water
4 ounces mixed dried apricots, prunes, peaches, and plums
(Serves 4)

Put meat in a saucepan with the beans and peas, beet, onion, spices, and salt. Add hot water, cover tightly, and simmer over low heat about 1 hour. Add dried fruit, cover, and simmer for 1 hour longer. Taste for flavor and if too sweet add 1 to 2 tablespoons lemon juice or verjuice or 3 to 4 crushed dried limes (*limu omani*—see Index).

APPLE AND SOUR CHERRY SOUP
(*Abgushte Sib*)

1 pound shank of mutton or veal
1 large onion, sliced
½ cup mixed yellow split peas and bleached wheat
2 cups hot water
½ teaspoon each turmeric and pepper
1 pound fresh cooking apples, peeled and chopped
2 tablespoons shortening
1 pound sour black cherries, pitted
1 teaspoon salt
½ tablespoon powdered mint leaves   (Serves 4)

Put meat in a saucepan with the onion, peas, and wheat. Add water and spices, cover tightly, and simmer over low heat about 1 hour. Sauté the apples in half the shortening with the cherries and salt for a few minutes, or until apple is partially tender. Add to the simmering meat, cover, and simmer about 1 hour longer. Just before serving, sauté the mint in the remaining oil and add to soup in serving bowl. Serve with herbs, radishes, and bread.

GIPA

This is a soup made of head, stomach, and trotters of lamb. It is one of the oldest soups in the history of Persian cuisine, dating back to the days of Bos-hac, who admired it repeatedly:

Years ago, before Moza'far [sweet polou] had bloomed
Among foods, as blooms yellow rose among flowers,
In my head I cherished yearning desire for Gipa.
Don't ask of Gipa and its concealed Secrets.
No one ever divulged this enigma, nor will ever do so!

The tradition of serving *Gipa* from 6 to 7 A.M. as an early, rich breakfast is still practiced among the peoples of small towns and villages, as it was in Bos-hac's days.

He who desires to have Gipa,
As early as dawn-breeze, he must awake!"

There are two kinds of *gipa*—one plain, the other elaborate. At the present time they are served as luncheon dishes.

PLAIN GIPA

(Serves 6)

Prepare one lamb's head, stomach, breast, and 2 to 4 trotters. Wash and clean thoroughly. Put all in a large deep saucepan with 2 large onions, chopped, and a piece of lamb fat. Add 1 teaspoon turmeric, a pinch of cloves, a bunch of fresh celery leaves, pepper, and sufficient water to cover. Then add 5 chopped dried limes (see Index), but no salt. Cover very tightly, first with a clean towel, then with the lid. Simmer over very low heat for 5 to 6 hours. When ready to serve, add salt to taste. A few pieces of chopped carrot may be added for flavor, if desired. Serving *gipa* with aromatic herbs, onions, radishes, and pickles is mandatory. Grapes served after *gipa* are traditional.

ELABORATE GIPA

(Serves 4)

Clean a head of lamb and put it in a deep pot with 2 onions, chopped, a few celery leaves, and ½ teaspoon each of pepper and turmeric. Add water to cover, cover pot, and simmer over low heat for 3 hours.

Meanwhile clean the stomach of a lamb and cut it into 2 parts, each as large as the palm of the hand. Sew three sides of the pieces together to form a small bag, leaving open about 3 inches at the top for the mouth of the bag.

Wash ⅓ pound rice and soak in ½ cup warm water for 30 minutes. Add ⅓ pound ground meat, 2 tablespoons sweetened tangerine- or orange-peel shreds (see Index), 4 tablespoons each chopped blanched almonds and shelled pistachios or walnuts, ½ teaspoon saffron, 5 to 6 dried chopped prunes or plums, and salt and pepper. Mix all together and stuff the bag with the mixture, leaving room at the top of the bag for the rice to expand as it cooks. Pour 2 tablespoons melted butter into the bag and sew mouth of bag closed.

Put bag in soup pot with the head, cover with a towel, then with the lid, and continue to simmer for 3 hours longer. When well cooked and the water has boiled down to a rich broth and the bag is soft and puffed, remove both head and bag from pan to a serving dish. Serve hot, and serve the broth separately. Herbs, radishes, and pickle are mandatory.

MEATLESS SOUP
(Eshkaneh)

(Serves 4)

Each part of the country has its favorite recipe for making *eshkaneh*. The basic ingredients are onion, flour, walnuts, and any kind of fruits, or fruit juice or yogurt as follows:

Sauté 1 onion, chopped, in 6 tablespoons cooking oil until onion is transparent. Stir in 2 tablespoons flour and cook, stirring, until flour is golden brown. Add ½ tablespoon powdered mint leaves, ½ teaspoon each of salt and pepper, and ½ cup coarsely chopped walnut meats and sauté for a few minutes longer. Then add any of the following ingredients: 2 cups pomegranate juice or 1 cup verjuice with ½ cup water, or 1 cup hot water and 1 pound pitted fresh sour black cherries or apricots and ½ cup sugar, or sugar to taste. Bring to a boil and simmer for 15 minutes. Drop in 4 eggs, one at a time, and simmer until the eggs are cooked. Serve hot with bread.

Yogurt may be used instead of fruit or juices. Stir in 1 cup yogurt and 1 sliced clove garlic, just before adding the eggs. Drop in eggs and stir very gently over low heat for 3 to 4 minutes.

HEAVY SOUPS
(Aashes)

Thick soups, similar to stews, are classic cold-weather dishes in all parts of Persia. They are ancient and hearty dishes, and are generally served for lunch.

Those who know how to make Aash,
Be sure, are great and ingenious artists.
Alive is the one in whose kitchen Aash is regularly served.

The varieties of *Aashes* are numerous in Iran, but here are a few which are popular with all.

YOGURT ASH
(Aashe Mast)

5 cups water
½ pound ground meat
1 large onion, minced
3 ounces yellow split peas
1 pound mixed fresh spinach, dill, and green onion tops, minced
½ teaspoon each pepper and turmeric
1 teaspoon salt
½ pound rice
2 cups yogurt
½ onion, finely chopped
2 tablespoons cooking oil
½ tablespoon powdered mint

(Serves 4 to 5)

Bring water to a boil in a deep saucepan. Add meat, onion, peas, vegetables, spices, and salt. Cover tightly and simmer over low heat for 30 minutes. Add rice and cook, covered, for 30 minutes longer, stirring occasionally to prevent the rice from sticking to the bottom of the pan, until all ingredients are well cooked. Stir in yogurt and heat, but be careful not to let the soup boil. Pour steaming soup into a tureen. Sauté the ½ finely chopped onion in the cooking oil until golden brown. Remove onion and sauté the mint for a few minutes in the oil remaining in the pan. When mint and oil turn green, sprinkle both fried onion and mint on top of the soup and serve hot.

POMEGRANATE ASH
(*Aashe Anar*)

 1 pound mixed fresh green onion tops, coriander, or parsley, minced
A few fresh mint leaves, minced
 1 large onion, minced
 1 medium beet, peeled and chopped
3 cups hot water
½ pound shoulder of lamb or veal with bone, chopped, or ground meat
3 ounces yellow split peas
½ teaspoon each pepper and turmeric
 1 teaspoon salt
½ pound rice
2 cups pomegranate juice

(Serves 4)

Put minced vegetables and chopped beet in a deep saucepan with the water. Add meat. If ground meat is used, form it into balls the size of small walnuts. Add peas, spices, and salt, cover tightly, and stir over medium heat for 15 minutes. Add rice and fruit juice, cover, and simmer for about 2 hours, stirring occasionally, until all ingredients are well cooked. If more liquid is needed during the cooking period, add 1 cup hot water or more fruit juice.

SOUR AASH
(Aashe Torsh)

The oldest recipes for the many varieties of *aash* are made with the juice of sour fruits and are considered to be remarkably effective health foods. Basically they are made in the same way as the pomegranate *aash*, but 2 pounds of fresh sour plums, prunes, or barberries or 2 cups of lemon juice are substituted for the pomegranate juice.

AASHE SAK

This is a refreshing thick soup which originated in the northern section of Persia and which is served in both summer and winter.

½ pound mixed lentils and red beans
1 large onion, chopped
5 cups hot water
½ pound ground meat
1 pound spinach, chopped
1 fresh beet, peeled and chopped
½ teaspoon each pepper, turmeric, and salt
2½ tablespoons rice flour (or wheat flour)
½ cup cold water
2 cups verjuice or ½ cup fresh lemon juice
4 eggs, lightly beaten
½ onion, minced
2 tablespoons cooking oil   (Serves 4)

Cook lentils, beans and chopped onion with the hot water in a deep saucepan for 15 minutes. Form the meat into balls and add to the boiling ingredients along with the spinach, beet, and spices. Cover tightly and simmer for 30 minutes. Combine flour and cold water, beating to a smooth paste, and stir into the boiling ingredients. Add the fruit juice and continue to cook for 30 minutes longer. When the mixture is rather thick, remove from fire and stir in the eggs. Pour into a tureen and garnish with the minced onion sautéed in the oil until golden.

WHEAT PORRIDGE
(Haleeme Gusht)

The remedy of my body and soul is Haleem,
Go, servant, and bring me that remedy!

(Serves 4)

This ancient dish, made only of wheat and meat, is indigenous to the cold parts of Persia. The meat must be of the very best and, in order of preference, goose, duck, or chicken first, venison second, and lamb last. *Haleem* originally was served as a breakfast food and even today entertaining at a *haleem* breakfast on cold winter mornings is a popular custom throughout Persia. It is also frequently served in winter for lunch, but never for dinner. *Haleem* is always sprinkled with hot butter and sugar or honey and is served with bread.

Trim off all fibers and skin from 2 pounds boneless shoulder of deer or lamb and cut into pieces. Put the meat in a heavy, deep saucepan with 1 whole onion and add enough hot water to cover the meat by a depth of 1 inch. Cover and bring to a boil, then simmer over low heat for 1 to 2 hours, or until meat is very tender. In another saucepan cook 1½ pounds bleached wheat in water to cover by a depth of 1 inch until tender. When wheat is soft, run it through the finest blade of a meat grinder.

Discard onion from meat and run the meat through the meat grinder. Mix wheat and meat and grind once more. Return mixture to the kettle and cook over low heat, stirring constantly, until cooked to a thick porridge.

If poultry is used, cook it whole, discard bones, and grind the meat. The amount of wheat should be equal to the weight of the fowl before it is cooked.

When ready to serve, turn mixture into a bowl. Heat a good quantity of butter, pour it over the *haleem*, and sprinkle with sugar or honey and lots of cinnamon. Serve with toasted bread. It is important that both the *haleem* and the butter be very hot. Pomegranates are traditionally served after *haleem*.

✑ Khoreshes
(*Stews*)

Happy is that Meat which is close to Butter and Walnut.
Delighted is that Pomegranate which has a secret with Sugar!

CLASSICAL AND SIMPLE KHORESHES
(Stews)

In Persia it is customary to serve *polous* and *chelous* with one of the many variety of *khoreshes*. The ones preferred, which are served at all important occasions, are: *Qa'meh, Qormeh Sabzi, Fesenjan,* and *Mosamma Bademjan,* which are centuries old.

All *khoreshes* are modestly spiced, but flavored with sour juices. The juices which may be used are either lime, lemon, sour orange, or verjuice. Sometimes dried pomegranate seeds are also used for flavoring.

The meats most often used for *khoreshes* are lamb, chicken, duck, or other fowl rich in fat.

There are also many varieties of *khoreshes* which are meatless, and I am giving some of the best ones in this book.

The usual spices used are saffron, black pepper, and turmeric, but for some *khoreshes* hot spices are required.

QA'MEH
(Finely Minced Meat)

Drops of butter on the face of Qa'meh
Tells us of the dews on tulip's petals.

This dish is mandatory at weddings, funerals, birthdays, at large dinner parties and religious public feasts. It is served with a sweet *polou* or *chelou*.

    1 large onion, chopped
    4 tablespoons butter or good oil
    1 pound ground lamb, veal, or beef
    ½ teaspoon pepper
    ½ teaspoon turmeric
    1 cup tomato juice
    ½ cup hot water
    ¼ pound dried yellow split peas
    ½ cup lime juice or 3 dried limes (limu omani)
    ½ teaspoon salt or to taste
    ¼ teaspoon saffron

Any of the following ingredients:

    ½ pound potatoes, chopped and fried
    1 eggplant, peeled and chopped
    ½ pound pitted sour cherries
    ½ pound fresh apples or quinces, chopped and fried
    4 ounces dried red (or small white) beans

Sauté the onion in the butter or oil in a deep pot until well browned. Remove onion and drain. In the butter remaining in the pot cook the meat, mixed with the pepper and turmeric. Stir well until all ingredients are smoothly mixed. Add tomato juice and hot water and cook over medium heat, covered, until meat is well done. Add split peas and lime juice or dried limes, and season to taste with salt. Partially cover and simmer over low heat for 45 minutes. Then add the fried onion and any of the other ingredients desired. Again partially cover and simmer until all ingredients are cooked and blended and a rich, colorful gravy rises to the surface. When ready to serve, pour into a serving bowl and top with ¼ teaspoon saffron mixed with a little hot water. One-half teaspoon of clove or curry powder may be added with the turmeric. In this case saffron is not used.

FESENJAN

This *khoresh* is also a very old and popular dish with all Iranians. It is mandatory at all festival dinners and the public food servings of the religious nights of Ramadan and Muharram. It may be made of duck, partridge, chicken, lamb or veal hind shin, shoulder, or ground meat.

1 large onion, minced
½ teaspoon pepper
½ teaspoon turmeric
2 tablespoons butter or cooking oil
1 pound meat or a small duck or partridge
1 tablespoon flour
½ pound walnut meats, coarsely chopped
⅓ cup hot water
1½ cups pomegranate juice*
Salt to taste
Juice of 1 or 2 lemons (optional)
1 small eggplant
Cooking oil
1½ teaspoons cardamom powder

(Serves 6)

Sauté the onion with the pepper and turmeric in the butter or the oil until well browned. Remove onion and drain. If ground meat is used, make small balls and brown slightly in the oil remaining in the pan. If birds are used, brown them on all sides.

Sprinkle meat or birds with the flour and the chopped walnuts and sauté for a few minutes longer. Add water, pomegranate juice, and salt to taste and, if you like a sourer dish, the lemon juice. Cover and simmer over low heat for 30 minutes.

Peel eggplant, cut lengthwise into 6 or 8 pieces, sprinkle each piece with salt, and stack one on top of the other for a few minutes to drain. Then rinse in cold water, dry, and sauté in hot oil until lightly browned on both sides. Arrange the eggplant on top of the meat or poultry, partially cover, and simmer over low heat until the eggplant is tender and a rich, brown gravy rises to the top. Add powdered cardamom, stir well but gently, and cook about 5 minutes longer. Serve with *chelo*.

NOTE: 1 pound white fish or salmon may be used instead of meat or poultry. In this case the cooking time will be about 15 minutes less. Also either of the following vegetables may be substituted for the eggplant: one pound fresh pumpkin meat, minced and sautéed, or one pound Italian squash, halved and sautéed.

* Sometimes I use lemon or lime juice, brown sugar, and ½ cup tomato juice when pomegranate juice is not available.

VEGETABLE KHORESHE
(*Qormeh Sabzi*)

This *khoresh* is served with *chelou* or *kateh*, *dami* and sweet *polou*. It is very much favored for picnics, and is humorously titled *say-yed-ul-qava-mire,* meaning the master of all minced ones.

    1 pound shoulder, leg, or shanks of lamb or veal with bone
    1 medium onion, chopped
    2 tablespoons oil
    1 teaspoon turmeric
    1 teaspoon black pepper
    ½ cup hot water
    1 cup lemon juice
    2 pounds equal parts of fresh green onion leaves, celery
        leaves, spinach, parsley, and fresh dill (if available)
    ⅓ cup any good oil

One of the following ingredients:
    3 ounces dried red or small white beans or ½ pound
        chopped raw potatoes

                                  (Serves 4 to 5)

Cut meat into large pieces and sauté it with the onion in the 2 tablespoons oil until browned. Add turmeric and pepper, the hot water, and lemon juice. Cover and cook over low heat for 10 minutes.

Meanwhile wash and mince all vegetable leaves and, without adding water, cook them in a large frying pan over low heat, folding constantly until wilted and dry. Add the ⅓ cup oil and mix and sauté about 5 minutes longer. Add vegetables to the simmering meat. If dried beans are to be used, they must be added now. Cover top partially and simmer over low heat for 30 minutes longer. If potatoes are used, they should be sautéed slightly in a little oil and then added to the meat. Let simmer again, partially covered, until a rich gravy rises to the top.

NOTE: Sour fruit such as unripe sour plums or dried limes may be added in place of the lemon juice.

EGGPLANT KHORESHE
(Mosamma Bademjan)

Eggplant is an important vegetable in Persian cuisine, and Persian cooks know how to make it appetizing. It is prepared for the table in many different ways. The most favorite is called *mosamma*, but it is also referred to as the *"khoresh* of kings and mullas," for it is believed that kings and Moslem priests always are served the choice dishes.

For many centuries *mosamma* has been the most popular of dishes. At formal dinners and elaborate parties, when one wishes to pay a compliment to the guest, it is always served along with a turkey or chicken *polou* or *chelou* or *dami* or *kateh.*

Serve with pickles or fresh limes.

2 large eggplants
2 large onions, sliced
¼ small green pepper, cut into rings
1 pound lamb or veal shoulder, hind shin, or shanks with the bone
OR 1 large chicken, cut into serving portions
4 large fresh tomatoes, peeled and chopped
Juice of 2 large lemons
Salt and pepper to taste
From ½–1 cup oil
½ teaspoon powdered saffron

(Serves 5 to 6)

Peel and cut eggplants lengthwise into 5 or 6 slices. Sprinkle the slices with salt and stack them to drain off the bitter juice. Arrange onion slices, green pepper slices, meat or chicken, and chopped tomatoes in alternate layers in a deep pot, finishing with tomatoes. Add lemon juice and seasoning, cover tightly, and simmer over low heat about 1 hour. When meat is well done, stir gently to mix all ingredients. Rinse eggplant and dry. Sauté the slices in hot oil until browned, soft, and glazed. Arrange the eggplant over the meat, partially cover, and cook over high heat for 15 minutes. Reduce heat to low and simmer until the eggplant is golden brown and the gravy is reduced to a brownish glaze. Stir only once, turn into large serving dish, and sprinkle with prepared saffron (see Index). The eggplant looks and tastes best when it is golden brown, not too dark in color.

Mosamma may be served with plain *chelou*, or the rice may be mixed with 2 ounces fried currants, ½ ounce toasted cuminseeds, and ½ teaspoon prepared saffron. These ingredients should be added after the rice is turned into the serving dish. Sliced tangerine peel, prepared as for sweet *polou*, may be used instead of the currants and cuminseeds. Italian squash may be substituted for the eggplant. In this case the dish is called *mosamma kadu.*

FRUIT AND NUT KHORESHE
(*Motanjen Khoreshe*)

8 ounces chopped blanched almonds, pistachios, or walnuts
1 pound boneless lamb or venison shoulder, ground
1 large onion, grated
½ teaspoon each salt and pepper
1 tablespoon butter or oil
¼ pound yellow split peas
1 cup hot water
1 pound mixed dried apricots, prunes, plums, and peaches
½ teaspoon powdered saffron

(Serves 6)

Sauté the nuts over very low heat in an ungreased pan until lightly browned. Mix meat with onion and salt and pepper and form into small balls. Cook throughout in a deep pot in the butter or oil until well browned on all sides. Add peas and water and cook, covered, over low heat for about 30 minutes, or until peas are soft. Wash fruits in hot water and add with the nuts. Salt to taste and simmer for 30 minutes longer. Sprinkle with prepared saffron (see Index). This *khoresh* should have a thick gravy. Shredded tangerine peel may also be added. This *khoresh* is usually served with *chelou, kateh,* or plain *dami.*

Easy Khoreshes

QUINCE KHORESHE
(*Khoreshe Beh*)

1 pound shoulder or hind shanks of lamb or veal with
    bone
1 large onion, minced
½ teaspoon each pepper and turmeric
¾ cup good cooking oil
1 cup hot water
3 ounces yellow split peas
2 large, ripe quinces
½ cup lemon juice
2 tablespoons molasses or brown sugar
Salt to taste

(Serves 5 to 6)

Trim the meat from the bones and mince it. Sauté the minced meat with the onion, pepper, and turmeric in 4 tablespoons of the oil until nicely browned. Add water and simmer, covered, for about 30 minutes. Add peas and continue to cook over low heat. Wash, peel, and slice or cube the quinces. Sauté in remaining oil until partially cooked and add to the meat. Add lemon juice and molasses or brown sugar (the exact amount depends on the cook's taste) and salt to taste. Simmer, partially covered, until a thick, rich, golden-brown gravy rises to the top. Serve with *dami, kateh, chelou,* or bread and pickles.

NOTE: Carrots may be used instead of quinces.

APPLE KHORESHE
(*Khoreshe Sib*)

1 pound roundsteak or veal, minced
4 tablespoons good cooking oil
1 cup hot water
1 pound apples, peeled and chopped
1 pound sour black cherries, pitted
½ cup lemon juice
Brown sugar to taste

(Serves 6)

Sauté the meat in 2 tablespoons of the oil until browned. Add water, cover, and simmer for about 30 minutes. Sauté the apples in remaining oil until partially soft and add to the meat along with the cherries. Continue to simmer, partially covered, over low heat for about 30 minutes longer, or until meat is tender. When nearly done, add the lemon juice and, if too sour, stir in as much brown sugar as desired. Serve with *chelou* or bread, *dami,* or *kateh.*

NOTE: 1 pound dried or 1½ pounds fresh plums or prunes may be substituted for the apples and cherries. If dried fruit is used, it must be added to the meat sooner than the fresh.

RASHTI KHORESHE

There are many varieties of this dish in different parts of Persia, but it originates among the people of northern Persia, especially in the city of Rasht. Here rice is cultivated, and their cuisine is based on *chelou,* which they serve with many kinds of fish and green vegetable *khoreshes.* The following recipe is one of them.

    1 pound boneless lamb or veal
    ½ teaspoon turmeric
    ½ teaspoon salt
    ½ teaspoon pepper
    ½ large onion, chopped
    4 tablespoons cooking oil
    2 cups hot water
    1 pound equal parts green onion tops, chives, and
        coriander leaves or celery leaves
    ½ teaspoon saffron

Discard the fat and fibers from the meat, cut meat into small pieces, and sauté with the turmeric, salt, pepper, and onion in half the oil until browned. Add the water, cover, and simmer for 30 minutes. Mince the greens and sauté in remaining oil until wilted, tossing constantly. Add to the meat, cover, and simmer for 30 minutes longer, or until meat is tender. Add prepared saffron (see Index) and serve with *chelou, kateh,* or *dami.*

CELERY KHORESHE
(Khoreshe Karafs)

1 pound hind shanks or round of lamb or veal, cut into
    large pieces
1 onion, chopped
½ teaspoon turmeric
1 teaspooon salt
½ teaspoon pepper
4 tablespoons cooking oil
2 cups hot water
A large bunch or 2 small bunches celery with the leaves
¼ pound fresh coriander leaves (or parsley)
1 small bunch mint (1 ounce), if desired
½ cup lemon juice
½ teaspoon saffron

(Serves 4 to 5)

Sauté the meat with the onion, turmeric, salt, and pepper
in half the oil until well browned. Add the water, cover, and
simmer for 15 minutes. Cut off and set aside the celery leaves
and cut the stalks into 4-inch pieces. Sauté them slightly.
Mince celery leaves, coriander or parsley, and the mint.
Sauté in remaining oil and add to the meat with the lemon
juice. Simmer for about 30 minutes, or until meat is partially
tender. Place celery pieces on top of meat and continue to
simmer over low heat for 30 minutes longer, or until meat is
tender and the gravy is rich. Add prepared saffron and serve
with *chelou, kateh,* or *dami* and fresh lime or lemon.

NOTE: Fresh green beans may be used instead of celery.
When using beans, add 1 cup tomato juice or 3 large tomatoes,
chopped, and no lemon juice.

RHUBARB KHORESHE
(Khoreshe Rivas)

1 pound boneless round or shoulder of lamb or veal
4 tablespoons butter or oil
1 cup water   Salt and pepper
1 pound fresh rhubarb, cut into 4-inch lengths
1 to 2 tablespoons brown sugar
Saffron

Sauté the meat in half the oil until well browned. Add
water and salt and pepper to taste, cover, and simmer for 45
minutes. Sauté the rhubarb in remaining oil for a minute and
add to meat. Stir in sugar mixed with a little hot water, cover
partially, and simmer for 15 to 20 minutes, or until fruit is
soft and the gravy is rich. If too sweet, add lemon juice; if too
sour, add more sugar. Do not stir while this *khoresh* is cooking.
When ready to serve, sprinkle with prepared saffron (see
Index). Serve only with *chelou, dami,* or *kateh.*

YOGURT KHORESHE
(Khoreshe Mast)

1 pound ground meat
1 teaspoon salt   ½ teaspoon pepper
½ teaspoon turmeric
3 tablespoons butter or oil
1 tablespoon curry powder
1 teaspoon clove (optional)
1 teaspoon cardamom (optional)
1 onion, grated
1 cup hot water
1 container yogurt   (Serves 4)

Make small meat balls of the ground meat mixed with the
salt, pepper, and turmeric. Sauté in the butter or hot oil

with the curry powder, clove, cardamom, and onion until well browned. Add water, cover, and simmer for 30 minutes. Stir in the yogurt and cook, uncovered, being careful it does not boil, for 5 minutes longer. Serve with *chelou, kateh,* or *dami.*

POMEGRANATE KHORESHE
(*Khoreshe Anar*)

This is another dish very popular in the northern parts of Persia.

    1 pound fresh coriander leaves or parsley
    1 ounce mint leaves
    6 tablespoons oil
    1 pound ground meat
    1 onion, minced
    ½ teaspoon pepper
    1 teaspoon salt
    ½ teaspoon turmeric
    ½ teaspoon clove (optional)
    8 ounces walnuts, coarsely chopped
    2 cups pomegranate juice

(Serves 4)

Mince the coriander or parsley and the mint leaves and sauté them in 3 tablespoons hot oil until wilted. Mix meat, onion, pepper, salt, turmeric, and clove and form tiny meat balls. Sauté in the remaining oil with onion until browned on all sides. Add to the vegetables. Add nuts and pomegranate juice and simmer, partially covered, about 1 hour, or until a rich gravy rises to the top. This dish does not need saffron. It is very delicious when served with *chelou, kateh,* or *dami.*

TANGERINE OR ORANGE-PEEL KHORESHE
(*Narange Khoreshe*)

1 pound lamb or veal hind shanks or shoulder
2 tablespoons butter or good cooking oil
½ teaspoon pepper
½ teaspoon turmeric
1 small onion, chopped
1 cup hot water
1 pound tangerine or orange peel
½ cup lemon juice
Salt to taste
½ teaspoon saffron

(Serves 4)

Chop meat into small pieces and sauté in the butter with the pepper, turmeric, and onion until lightly browned. Add hot water, cover, and simmer for 30 minutes. Prepare the tangerine or orange peel according to instructions (see Index), only cut the peel into 2-inch pieces. Add peel to the meat with the lemon juice and salt and simmer for 15 minutes longer. When well done and gravy is rich, add prepared saffron and serve with *chelou, kateh,* or *dami.*

NOTE: 2 pounds okra may be used instead of the peels. Cut off the stems and fry in a little butter or shortening until partially cooked. Add to half-cooked meat with 1 cup tomato juice or 1 pound chopped fresh tomatoes. Do not add saffron or lemon juice, and do not stir when okra is added.

Meatless Khoreshes

There are many vegetable *khoreshes* without meat which are served with bread or rice. Some of these are:

FRIED EGGPLANT KHORESHE
(*Bademjan Sorkh Kardeh*)

This is a very popular dish and a favorite with all Persians. It appears frequently on everyday menus in Persian homes.

    1 large eggplant
    ½ cup oil
    ½ pound tomatoes, peeled and thinly sliced
    ⅓ cup hot water

(Serves 4)

Peel the eggplant and cut lengthwise or into thin rounds. Sprinkle the slices generously with salt and stack them in a pile to drain for 10 minutes. Then rinse in cold water and dry. Sauté the eggplant in the hot oil until glazed and golden on both sides, adding more oil if needed. Arrange the tomato slices over the eggplant. Add the hot water and cook, uncovered, over medium heat for 30 minutes, or until the eggplant is soft and glazed with a rich, brown gravy.

If this dish is to be served with bread, grate half an onion into a cup of wine vinegar. Add salt and black pepper to taste, then either pour it over the food in the serving dish or serve it in a separate gravy bowl for people to help themselves to the quantity they wish. This dish must be served hot, otherwise it loses flavor.

SWOONED PRIEST
(Mollah Ghash Kardeh)

This dish is so delicious that even mulla is supposed to faint from the sheer joy of eating it!

2 large onions, sliced
3 large tomatoes, sliced
1 eggplant, peeled and sliced ½ inch thick
Salt and pepper
1 small bunch of fresh coriander or parsley, minced
⅓ cup hot water
2 tablespoons oil
2 cloves garlic, sliced

(Serves 3 to 4)

Arrange onions, tomatoes, and eggplant in alternate layers in a frying pan, sprinkling each layer with salt and pepper and the minced greens. Add water, oil, and garlic. Cover tightly and simmer for about 30 minutes or until the liquid is reduced to a rich gravy. Serve hot either with bread or *chelou, dami* or *kateh.*

THE SIX FALLEN
(Shesh Andaze)

Grate 1 pound of any one of the following fruits or vegetables: Quinces, apples, carrots, or potatoes. Sauté the fruit or vegetable in ¼ cup butter or hot oil in a large frying pan until partially cooked. To apples, quinces, or carrots, add ½ cup lemon juice. To potatoes add only ⅓ cup hot water. Sprinkle with salt and pepper, cover, and simmer for 15 minutes. Then spread the fruit or vegetable into a smooth layer in the same pan and make 6 indentations in the top. Drop an egg into each indentation and cook until the eggs are hard. Serve two eggs with the surrounding vegetable or fruit to each person. Serve with *chelou* or bread. Spinach may also be used, but this does not require further cooking after it is fried.

✍ Kababs
(Broiled Meals and Vegetables)

Though chicken broils, and salt brings tears into its eyes,
The sight of it delights my heart—what a joy!
Here comes delicious fragrance from the kitchen.

In the Persian language *kabab* means simply broiled meat,
yet there are many methods of preparing it, each part of the
country having its own specialty. Since the climate varies
greatly in different parts of Iran, from the fertile green pastures
of the lowlands to the high mountains, many varieties of animals, both wild and domestic, are abundant throughout the
land, and the flesh of these animals and birds is used in different regions in the making of *kababs*.

For uncountable generations *kababs* have been a favorite
food for both parties and for picnics, and Persian cooks know
how to make them savory and inviting. An old tradition always
associates *kababs* and wine or other alcoholic beverages, and
in Persian literature the two words *kabab* and *sharab* (wine)
are always found together.

Although *kababs* are the favorite method of preparing meat
all through the Middle East, the recipes given in this book are
typically Persian. All kinds of fragrant herbs and aromatic
pickles, salads, and radishes are served with *kababs*.

CHELOU KABAB

This *kabab* is made especially for serving with *chelou* and
must be tender and juicy. The *chelou*, too, must be feathery,

very white, and delicate in flavor. *Chelou Kabab* is not only popular with all Persians but is one of the dishes most enjoyed by visitors from abroad. In the Shamshiri restaurant in Tehran the very best *chelou Kabab* is served today. Everyone, including our foreign visitors, frequents this restaurant for lunch and dinner. If it happens that you, too, should visit Tehran someday, do not fail to go there and judge for yourself the difference between *chelou kabab* of Persia and the popular American counterpart known as shish kebab.

The finest *kababs* are made from top-quality fillet or top round of lamb or venison, although often boneless chuck, sirloin, and even rump or shoulder are used.

There are two different kinds of *chelou kabab*, the first known as:

LEAF KABAB
(*Kababe Barg*)

2 pounds fillet or top round
4 onions, grated
1 cup fresh lemon juice
Salt and pepper

(Serves 6 to 8)

Remove all fibers from the meat and cut into thin slices about 3 inches wide and 4 inches long. Beat each slice gently with the sharp edge of a knife several times in order to make fine cuts in the pieces, but be careful not to cut them all the way through. Place the meat in a china dish and cover with the grated onion. Add lemon juice and store in refrigerator for 12 hours to 3 days. About 20 minutes before serving remove meat and brush off onion. Sprinkle with salt and pepper. Stick two skewers into each piece from either side to keep the pieces flat, and broil over flaming charcoal or under broiler flame, turning skewers frequently until the meat is brown on all sides. It must be juicy and not over-cooked.

The second method of making *chelou kabab* is called

ROLLED KABAB
(*Luleh Kababe*)

1½ pounds lean meat, ground twice
3 onions, grated
Salt and pepper
½ teaspoon saffron
2 egg yolks

(Serves 4 to 5)

Put the meat in a china bowl and cover with grated onions. Cover bowl and leave in refrigerator to marinate for several hours. About 20 minutes before serving, remove meat from the juice, brushing off the onion, and rub with salt and pepper, the prepared saffron, and the egg yolks. Wet skewers with a little water and shape the ground meat around them in cylinders, pressing the meat tightly around the skewers so that it sticks tightly. The meat cylinders must be a little shorter in length than the skewers themselves. Broil over flaming charcoal or under the broiler flame, although charcoal is much to be preferred. If charcoal is used, turn skewers round and round frequently over the fire until the *kababs* are browned on all sides, but still juicy.

SERVING THE CHELOU KABABS

There is a special way to serve either of the above two *kababs*. In the first place a white, feathery *chelou* is mandatory and must be hot and ready to serve. Then shake out the white from one or two eggs per serving through a hole made in the top of each shell, leaving the yolks in the shells. Put the shells holding the yolks in a dish on the table near the *kababs* and *chelou*. Each person places a portion of rice on his own plate with a large pat of sweet butter and one or two egg yolks in the center of the hot rice. The rice is then sprinkled with salt and pepper and dried powdered sumac fruit,* and eaten with the hot *kababs*. Remember that both the *chelou* and the *kababs* must be served hot—the hotter the more delicious. If served lukewarm, they lose much of their appeal and flavor.

Some people like sliced raw onions with their *kababs*. The beverage which usually accompanies *chelou kabab* is *doogh*, which is a popular, cooling drink for hot summer days. Yogurt or sour milk is poured into a wide-mouthed bottle and shaken for a couple of hours. All the butter in the sour milk or yogurt separates and is removed. The resulting liquid is the *doogh*. It is frequently served with ice and is enjoyed by the Persians in much the same way as Americans love orange juice. It will keep in the refrigerator for days. Americans might prefer to substitute buttermilk or diluted yogurt.

---

* One particular genus of sumac tree grows in abundance in Persia. It has pyramidal panicles of small crimson, one-seed, sour fruits which are dried, powdered, and sold in the markets. This fruit has many uses in Persian foods and is also used medicinally. But in America sumac is used only for tanning and dyeing. There is no substitute for this seasoning with *chelou kabab*.

CUT PIECES KABAB
(Kenjeh Kababe)

This is the kabab that the Turks call sheshlik. In America the two words—the Turkish *sheshlik* and the Persian *kenjeh-kabab*—have become confused and combined to make *shesh-kabab*, or shish kebab!

Kenjeh kabab is served with either *chelou* or with bread and salads, pickles, or with yogurt dishes called *borani*, of which I shall talk later. Fragrant herbs such as sweet basil, marjoram, and mint, and also red radishes and fresh onions and chives are always served with it.

2 pounds lamb or veal, sirloin, rump, or shoulder
3 large onions
1 cup fresh lime juice
Salt and pepper
½ teaspoon saffron

(Serves 6)

Remove all the heavy fibers from the meat and cut the meat into 2-inch cubes. Grate onions into a deep china bowl and add the lime juice. Soak meat in the mixture, partially covered, in the refrigerator for 2 or 3 days, stirring the pieces once a day, which helps to make them tender. About 30 minutes before serving, take meat out of the juice and clean off the onion. Season pieces well with salt, pepper, and prepared saffron. Insert skewers through the pieces, keeping each piece close to the other and inserting a small piece of lamb fat between them. Broil over a very hot charcoal fire or under the broiler, turning the skewers frequently until meat is browned on all sides, but still juicy. One cup yogurt may be used in place of the lime juice. This *kabab* is the favorite for picnics.

BIRD KABAB
(Kababe Parandeh)

Great is the ecstasy of my heart, caused by
The breast of goose, the drumstick of hen, and
The breast of partridge!

There are many types of birds that may be used for making this *kabab*—chicken, partridge, pheasant, squab, or any other fowl tender and rich in fat. It used to be the custom in the winter to bury the fowl in the snow, complete with feathers, for two days in order to tenderize and age it. In the summertime it was soaked for about half a day in the cold, fresh water of the pool. But now, with refrigeration, these processes are unnecessary.

If the bird is small and tender, it may simply be pierced by two skewers and brushed generously with a mixture of half cooking oil or melted butter and half lemon juice. It is then broiled over a blazing charcoal flame until done. During the broiling period it is turned frequently and basted often with the oil and juice mixture. Partridge and squab are delicious broiled in this manner.

But if the bird is large and one suspects its succulence, it is first stewed in a tightly covered pot with 1 whole onion and about ⅓ cup water until tender. It is then broiled as above.

Bird *kababs* are served with any fresh aromatic herb or with salad greens, and usually with fresh radishes and a sour pickle.

CHICKEN KABAB
(Kababe Morgh)

Cut a large chicken into serving portions. Wash and put the pieces into a deep saucepan with ¼ cup hot water, 1 small whole onion, a few peppercorns, ½ cup lemon juice, and 1 large tomato, sliced. Cover and bake in a moderate oven (350°) or over low heat until tender. Remove chicken and sprinkle with 2 tablespoons melted butter or oil. Season with salt and pepper and broil under the broiler, or insert skewers through the pieces and broil over charcoal flame, turning frequently until golden brown. Serve with bread, salad, pickles, radishes, green onions, fresh herbs and drinks.

CHICKEN KABAB WITH FRUIT

Stuff a large chicken or cock with 2 small onions, 2 tablespoons each of dried barberries and currants, 1 ounce of dried limes (limu omani), salt, pepper, and a pinch of clove. Sew up the opening and put chicken in a deep saucepan with ½ cup lemon juice, ½ cup tomato juice, and ½ teaspoon prepared saffron. Bake, covered, in a moderate oven (350°) until almost tender. Remove and insert two large skewers—one from each end—and broil over blazing charcoal, turning frequently, or in a rotisserie oven, basting occasionally with melted butter or oil. Serve with herbs, salad, yogurt, or pickle, and drinks.

POT KABAB
(Kababe Dig)

Although this meat dish is not broiled at all, but is baked

or roasted, it has been known for generations as "*kabab* in a pot."

> 1 large roast of meat—lamb or veal shoulder, leg or round
> 1 clove garlic
> 1 small carrot, sliced
> 2 small stalks celery
> 2 large onions
> 2 large tomatoes
> Salt and pepper
> ½ teaspoon turmeric
> ½ cup lemon juice or sour-orange juice
> ¼ cup butter or margarine or any good oil
> ½ teaspoon saffron

Wipe meat with a damp cloth. Make a few small slits in the flesh here and there and insert thin slices of garlic. Place meat in a large, deep pot with the carrot, celery, onion, tomatoes, salt, pepper, turmeric, and ¼ cup of the sour juice. Cover tightly and bake in a preheated 350° oven for 2 to 3 hours, depending on size of roast. Check every 20 minutes and add a very little hot water if the juice has cooked away. When meat is well done and liquid has cooked away, place pot over low heat and add the butter and remaining sour juice. Sauté until the meat is browned and there is a small quantity of brown gravy in the pan. Place meat on a large serving dish and sprinkle with prepared saffron (see Index). Surround by the pan gravy, aromatic herbs, and radishes.

LAMB KABAB
(*Kababe Barreh*)

This is also one of the oldest types of *kababs,* and there are two methods of preparing it. The primitive method is still used by villagers and nomads of Persia and is extremely simple and delicious:

Remove the skin from a whole baby lamb. Clean lamb and wash thoroughly inside and out. Then season with salt and pepper, replace it in the skin and sew up. Make a very strong fire with plenty of wood either over a heap of tiny pebbles or over a hole dug in sandy ground. When the fire burns down to a hot ash, place the lamb under the heap of pebbles or in the hot sand and leave it for half a day until it is well baked and tender.

The modern method, which is used by the city folk, is as follows:

Combine ½ pound of mixed dried fruits and nuts—plums, prunes, peaches, half-ripe dates, currants, raisins, apricots, blanched almonds, walnut meats, hazelnuts or pistachios (you may use any or all of these ingredients)—with ½ teaspoon each of pepper, turmeric, and cloves, 5 dried limes, powdered, ½ teaspoon prepared saffron, (cardamom and cinnamon are also frequently used for flavor) and 2 tablespoons shredded tangerine peel. Sauté the mixture for a few minutes in 2 tablespoons butter or good oil and then use it to stuff the inside of a tiny baby lamb. Sewing is not necessary.

Place lamb in a large roasting pan with 1 cup lemon or sourorange juice and 2 cups tomato juice. Cover tightly and bake in a preheated 350° oven until very tender. Serve with *polou* mixed with saffron and cuminseeds, or with salad, bread, sliced fresh onion, fresh mint or other herbs, radishes, and wine.

Large chicken, pheasant, or any kind of large bird such as duck or goose may be stuffed and baked as above until tender. The bird is also sautéed in butter or oil until browned on all sides, if desired.

FISH KABAB
(Kababe Mahi)

A whole fish may be stuffed with the same fruits and nuts as given for *kababe barreh*. The head and tail are brought together and sewed in place. The fish is then broiled over charcoal or put into a large, deep, covered saucepan and baked.

To bake the fish, place a few small clean sticks crosswise in the bottom of the pan (or use a trivet) and place the fish on the sticks. Pour over ½ cup lemon juice mixed with ½ teaspoon prepared saffron, cover and bake in a preheated 350° oven until tender, basting several times with juices in pan.

KIDNEY AND HEART KABAB
(Kababe Kolbeh)

This is a simple *kabab* which is often served at picnics or at family meals with a bottle of wine or other beverage.

Cut 1 calf heart, 4 lamb kidneys, and 1 small calf's liver into medium-sized chunks, sprinkle them with 2 grated onions, a generous amount of freshly ground pepper, and a little poultry seasoning. Let stand for 2 hours. Pierce skewers through pieces of meat, alternating heart, kidney, and liver and placing a thin slice of onion between each two pieces. Broil over blazing charcoal, turning constantly. When meat begins to drip, sprinkle with salt and continue to turn until well broiled and browned on all sides. Serve hot with bread.

SHAMI KABAB

O Cook! You delight my heart with Shami
And I add a hundred coins to your Salary.

A favorite for luncheon parties and formal dinners as well as for family meals, *shami kabab* is served either hot or cold accompanied by bread, all sorts of salads and pickles, or yogurt mixed with minced cucumber or spinach (see *borani*), or with plain yogurt sprinkled with chopped onions and chives. Sliced onions, radishes, fresh mint leaves, sweet basil, fresh marjoram or tarragon and romaine leaves with vinegar are commonly served with it. Most of the countries in the Middle East—Turkey, Armenia, and Arabia—all have their own indigenous variations of this *kabab*.

    1 pound short ribs of lamb, veal, or venison
    1 large onion, minced
    1 teaspoon each salt, turmeric, and cloves
    ¼ cup hot water
    ¾ pound yellow split peas
    ½ cup water
    ½ pound lean beef or lamb, ground
    5 eggs, beaten
    ½ teaspoon saffron
    1 pint cooking oil or 1 pound shortening

(Serves 4)

Cook the short ribs with the onion, salt, turmeric, cloves, and the ¼ cup hot water in a small pot until all the water has boiled away. Wash peas and cook in the ½ cup water for about 20 minutes, then add to the meat and continue to cook until the peas are very soft and the water has cooked away.

Take the meat from the bones and mix meat, peas, and ground raw meat together. Pound well with a meat hammer or potato masher until well blended, then knead in the eggs. Add the prepared saffron and let the mixture stand in the refrigerator for 2 to 3 hours. Then knead again thoroughly.

Wet a fine clean cloth and place it over a large saucer or bowl, which is used to mold the patty. Dust mold with flour.

Take a ball of the mixture as big as a walnut and spread it over the wet cloth, making a round patty about ½ inch thick, and sprinkling with a little flour to prevent meat from sticking to the hand. Make a hole in the center of the cake with a finger. Heat the shortening in a large flat pan and in it fry the patties, a few at a time. The hot shortening must cover the patty. As soon as the patties are brown and crisp, remove to a paper towel to drain.

If the dough is too soft and the patty breaks into pieces during the frying, sprinkle a little more flour over the cloth when molding the patties.

Red beans may be substituted for the yellow split peas.

BOWL KABAB
(Tas Kababe)

This is a famous Persian dish, especially favored for picnics. There are many variations of it, made of fruit and vegetables such as okra, eggplant, squash, quinces, apples, prunes, and plums.

        2 large onions, sliced
        3 large tomatoes, sliced
        ¼ green pepper, chopped
        1 pound round or shoulder of lamb or veal, cubed
        ¼ cup oil, or a few pieces of lamb fat
        1 cup lemon juice or 2 cups pomegranate juice or sour-
            orange juice
        1 eggplant
        ½ teaspoon each saffron, turmeric, and pepper
        A pinch of cloves

(Serves 4)

Arrange alternate layers of onion slices, half the tomato slices, the green pepper, and the meat in a deep saucepan and place remaining tomato slices on top. Add oil or lamb fat, half the juice and spices. Cover tightly and simmer over low heat for 1 hour, or until meat is tender.

Meanwhile peel and slice the eggplant. Sprinkle the slices generously with salt, stack them, and let drain for 15 minutes.

When meat is tender, rinse and dry the eggplant slices and sauté them slightly in a little oil. Place the eggplant on top of the other ingredients, add remaining juice, cover partially, and continue to simmer for 20 minutes longer or until a thick, rich gravy rises to the top. Stir occasionally, very gently in order to mix only the ingredients beneath the eggplant slices. Sprinkle with prepared saffron and serve hot with *chelou, dami,* or bread, pickles and herbs, and radishes.

All other fruits and vegetables mentioned above are cooked in the same way as the eggplant. And all of them may be combined together, making a very delicious *tas kabab,* or *"tas kabab* of Gamblers."

✍ Kuftehs
(Meat Balls)

Ground meat, formed into balls and cooked in a variety of ways, appears frequently in the daily menu of the Persian people. It would be impossible to attempt to give recipes for the many variations, as each housewife adds something of her own preference in seasonings and ingredients to a favorite recipe. I have selected only two, which I feel are representative of the best and most unusual in Persian cooking. *Kuftehs* are usually served with bread, fresh onions, radishes, herbs, yogurt, or pickles.

THE BIGGEST BALLS
(*Kufteh Mo'alla*)

This *kufteh* is usually served only for parties or for private guests.

> 1 pound lamb shoulder, ground
> 2 large onions
> ½ pound split peas
> ½ pound rice
> 1 small bunch each fresh dill, green onions, chives, and coriander or marjoram or parsley
> ¼ cup butter or oil
> Spices to taste—salt, pepper, clove
> ½ teaspoon saffron
> 2 ounces dried currants and barberries

2 ounces prunes or plums
2 tablespoons shredded tangerine peel (see Index)
5 hard-cooked eggs
4 tablespoons shelled pistachios
4 tablespoons chopped blanched almonds or walnuts
½ small onion, chopped and sautéed in butter until lightly
    browned
1 pound lamb bones
6 cups water
Salt and pepper
½ teaspoon turmeric
2 ounces (4 tablespoons) rice, pounded
½ cup lemon juice
¼ teaspoon saffron or curry powder
Brown sugar
½ tablespoon powdered mint
1 tablespoon oil

(Serves 4 to 5)

Grind meat and 1 large onion twice through finest blade of a meat grinder. Cook peas with water until tender. Cook rice according to directions for *chelou* and rinse. Wash the green herbs, mince very fine, and sauté in butter or oil until wilted. Combine meat, peas, rice, and herbs and pound well with a meat hammer or potato masher. Add spices and ½ teaspoon prepared saffron and knead until the meat dough is well blended.

Moisten the inside of a large bowl, to serve as a mold, with 1 tablespoon cold water. Press half the meat into the bowl. In the center place the currants, barberries, prunes, half the tangerine shreds, 3 of the hard-cooked eggs, the pistachios and chopped nuts, and the fried onion. Put remaining meat on top and form all into one large ball.

Simmer the lamb bones in the water with the other large onion and salt and pepper and turmeric for about 1 hour. Remove bones and put the meat ball in the broth. There must be sufficient liquid to cover the ball; if not, add as much water as needed. Add the pounded rice and cover and simmer for about 1 hour, or until meat ball is well done. Add lemon juice, the ¼ teaspoon saffron or curry, and remaining tangerine shreds, and sweeten the broth to taste with brown sugar. Simmer, covered, for 5 minutes longer.

Sauté the mint in the 1 tablespoon oil.

Place the meat ball in a large serving dish and pour the broth over it. Sprinkle with the fried mint and the remaining 2 hard-cooked eggs, chopped. Serve the soup separately.

Garnish with a few leaves of fresh coriander, sweet basil, or parsley. Serve hot or cold with any pickles desired.

MEAT BALLS OF TABRIZ
(Kufteh Tabrizi)

Tabriz is the capital of Azerbaijan province in northern Persia.

  ½ pound rice
  ¼ pound yellow split peas
  1 pound ground lamb, veal, or beef
  2 onions, grated
  ¼ teaspoon each turmeric, pepper, and curry or clove
  ½ teaspoon salt
  3 hard-cooked eggs or 6 to 9 dried prunes or plums
  12 almonds, blanched and chopped
  1 large onion, chopped and sautéed in butter until lightly
      browned

(Serves 3)

Cook the rice according to directions for *chelou* and rinse. Cook peas until very tender, then mash. Grind the meat twice through finest blade of a meat grinder. Combine the rice, peas, meat, grated onion, spices, and salt and knead the mixture into a dough. Wet a clean cloth and spread it in a small round bowl, approximately 6 inches in diameter, which will serve as a mold. Fill the bowl half full of dough. In the center place either a hard-cooked egg or 3 prunes or plums, and sprinkle with a little chopped almonds and 1 teaspoon of the sautéed onion. Cover the ingredients with more of the meat dough and shape the whole into a medium-sized ball. Make two more balls in the same manner, using remaining ingredients.

Bring to a boil 3 quarts of water, filling to the top a saucepan large enough to hold the three meat balls. Add remaining sautéed onion and carefully lower the meat balls into the boiling water. Cover and simmer for about 2 hours, or until well done. Remove meat balls to a serving dish and either pour the broth over them or serve it separately.

If desired, 2 cups lemon or pomegranate juice may be substituted for part of the water used to cook the balls. Also cooked chicken meat, mixed with fruit and nuts, may be used in the center of the meat balls in place of eggs.

✐ Dolmehs
(Stuffed Dishes)

Among the many Persian dishes and delicacies which have been adopted by neighboring countries are the various *Dolmehs,* or stuffed vegetable dishes, which are popular not only with the Persians but with the Turks, the Arabs, Indians, and Armenians. The recipes following are typical Persian recipes.

EGGPLANT DOLMEH
(*Dolmeh Bademjan*)

Basic Stuffing
- 5 tablespoons rice
- ⅓ pound ground meat
- 1 onion, grated
- ½ teaspoon each of saffron, pepper, turmeric, clove, and salt
- 4 tablespoons butter or oil
- A small bunch fresh coriander or parsley
- A few fresh onion leaves
- 3 tablespoons yellow split peas
- 2 large eggplants
- 1 cup lemon juice, or sour-orange juice
- Brown sugar to taste

(Serves 3 to 4)

Boil rice according to directions given for *chelou,* drain, and reserve the water. Sauté the meat with the onion and spices in

1 tablespoon of the butter or oil until meat is browned. Mince the parsley and onion leaves fine. Cook split peas in a little water for 5 minutes, drain, and mix with the meat, rice, and greens. Salt to taste and mix well.

Cut off about 1 inch from the tops of the eggplants and set aside to use later for covers. Peel and fry the eggplants on all sides in 2 tablespoons of the butter or oil until partially tender. Then scoop out the insides of the eggplants very carefully so as not to break through the skin, leaving a shell about ½ inch thick. Chop the removed part of the eggplant and combine with meat mixture. Fill the eggplants with the mixture, pressing it into the hollows gently so that the eggplants will not break. Replace tops, securing them with toothpicks, and place the eggplants upright in a large deep pan. Add 1 cup drained rice water or hot water and the lemon juice. The liquid should reach more than halfway up the sides of the eggplants. Add as much brown sugar as desired and the remaining butter or oil. Cover tightly and simmer over very low heat about 1 hour, or until most of the water is cooked away, the stuffing is well cooked, and a thick, rich gravy covers the bottom of the pan. Serve with bread, sliced fresh onion, radishes, and fresh herbs.

ELABORATE EGGPLANT DOLMEH

In this favorite *dolmeh* the eggplants are not peeled and the rice (4 tablespoons) is sautéed before it is cooked in 6 tablespoons good oil with 3 tablespoons raisins or currants, ¼ pound ground meat, and a small bunch of dill or parsley, finely chopped. Then add enough hot water to cover the rice about 1 inch deep, cover first with a towel and then with the lid, and simmer over very low heat about 30 minutes, or until all the water is absorbed. Remove and stir in ½ teaspoon each of cardamom, cinnamon, salt, and pepper, and 1 small onion, chopped and sautéed in 2 tablespoons oil until lightly browned. Scoop out the insides of the eggplants, chop pulp, blend with meat mixture, and stuff the eggplants. Use either 2 large eggplants or 4 small, and cook as in the recipe above. Serve hot.

STUFFED GRAPE LEAVES
(Dolmeh Barg)

(Serves 4 to 5)

The stuffing ingredients for this recipe are exactly the same as those used in *dolmeh bademjan*. Grape leaves are used instead of eggplant.

Wash fresh, tender grape leaves (or those preserved in brine) and put as much stuffing in the center of each as the leaf will hold when folded. If the leaves are small, use two overlapping. Then fold corners of the leaf over the filling and tie each little bundle with string.

Arrange the bundles in a deep saucepan, one on top of the other to form a mound. Either arrange a layer of fresh greengage plums between each layer of *dolmehs*, or pour ½ cup lemon juice or 2 cups verjuice over all. Add 3 tablespoons melted butter or other good shortening and as much water as needed to cover the *dolmehs* to two thirds of their depth. Season with salt and pepper and press a small, flat, metal piepan or aluminum dish on top of the *dolmehs*. Place a stone or other weight on the dish to hold the *dolmehs* under the liquid while they are cooking. Cover tightly and cook over very low heat until most of the liquid has cooked away and the leaves and stuffing are juicy and tender. Turn off heat, but leave the *dolmehs* covered for about 30 minutes. Then arrange them in a serving dish, removing the strings. This *dolmeh* is preferably served cold with drinks.

TOMATO DOLMEH

(Serves 4 to 5)

Prepare basic stuffing as given in recipe for *dolmeh badem-jan*. Cut the tops off 4 or 5 large, ripe tomatoes, saving the tops to use as covers over the stuffing. Scoop out insides of tomatoes, leaving a shell ½ inch thick. Chop removed tomato and add to the meat mixture. Fill the tomatoes with the stuffing, replace tops, and secure with toothpicks. Arrange the tomatoes in a small deep saucepan, with a sprinkling of finely minced coriander or parsley and salt and pepper over each. Add ¼ cup tomato juice and 3 tablespoons melted butter or good oil, cover tightly, and cook over low heat about 30 minutes, or until juice is cooked down to a rich gravy and the tomatoes are soft and juicy. Serve hot.

Large green peppers are frequently cooked in the same manner, but first hold them, one at a time, over a flame, turning constantly, until the peel bursts in several places. Remove peel, cut off tops, and discard the seeds, or mix some of the seeds into the stuffing. Continue as in the above recipe.

STUFFED PASTRY
(*Kotab Dolmeh*)

½ package active dry yeast
1 cup rose water, orange-flower water, or water
4 cups (1 pound) sifted flour
½ teaspoon cardamom
¼ cup melted butter or any good cooking oil
1 cup lentils
1 small onion, grated
6 tablespoons oil
Oil for frying

Soften the yeast in the flower water. Add flour and cardamom and stir in the butter or oil to make a dough. Turn out on a lightly floured board and knead until smooth. Cover with a towel and let rise in a warm place for about 2 hours.

Meanwhile cook the lentils in water to cover until soft and most of the liquid has cooked away. Mash the lentils until smooth, combine with the onion, and sauté in the 6 table-spoons oil until golden brown.

Punch down the dough and roll it out on a lightly floured board until it is 1 inch thick. Cut it into round loaves 3 inches in diameter. Spread half of each round generously with the lentil paste, fold in half, and press edges together, moistening the edges with water if necessary to make them secure. Fry the little loaves in deep hot shortening until both sides are puffed and browned and cooked through to the center. Serve hot. It is very delicious if brown sugar or molasses is added to the lentil paste.

STUFFED QUINCE
(Dolmeh Beh)

⅓ pound ground beef
1 onion, minced
2 tablespoons yellow split peas
2 tablespoons cooked rice
¼ small cauliflower, finely chopped
½ teaspoon turmeric
1 teaspoon salt
¼ cup chopped walnut meats
2 large, ripe, yellow quinces
2 tablespoons cooking oil
3 cups pomegranate juice or ½ cup lemon juice and 1 cup
   hot water

(Serves 3 to 4)

Sauté the beef with the minced onion in a little oil until browned. Cook peas in water to cover for 5 minutes and drain. Combine meat, peas, rice, cauliflower, turmeric, salt, and walnuts, and sauté all together for a few minutes in the oil remaining in the pan.

Cut tops from the quinces and scoop out the centers, leaving a shell about one inch thick. Stuff the hollows with the meat mixture, replace tops, and fasten with toothpicks. Place the quinces upright in a large saucepan with the oil and add the liquid to cover fruit by two thirds. Cover with a towel and then with lid, and cook over low heat for 2 hours, or until quinces are well done and soft and a small amount of rich brown gravy remains in the saucepan. Serve hot with bread.

𝒮 Kukus
(Egg Dishes)

"Oh, who could remain calm and patient,
And his heart reposing, when I talk
Of the attributes of hot Kukus!

A popular ancient dish of Persia, called *kuku*, is easily made with beaten eggs mixed with vegetables, meat, or fish. There are many variations to the basic recipe, but one of the favorites, served at formal dinners, weddings, and receptions is . . .

VEGETABLE KUKU
(*Kukuye Sabzi*)

6 eggs
1 small onion, grated
1 tablespoon flour
1 pound mixed fresh coriander or parsley, chives, green
   onion tops, romaine leaves, and dill, all finely minced
½ teaspoon each pepper, salt, and saffron
½ cup cooking oil

(Serves 4 to 5)

Beat eggs until light and fluffy. Add onion, flour, and minced vegetables and season with spices. In an 8-inch frying pan heat oil until very hot. Pour in egg mixture, cover, and bake in a preheated 350° oven for 30 minutes. Check underside of the *kuku* by lifting edge with the blade of a knife. If well browned and the top well puffed, cut it into quarters and turn each piece upside down. Cover and continue cooking for 10 minutes longer, or until brown on other side. Remove from oven and place *kuku* in a flat dish. Serve hot or cold with *chelou* or bread. If it is served with *chelou,* sprinkle it with 2 or 3 tablespoons of *chelou* for decoration. Six ounces chopped walnut meats or 2 ounces dried barberries may be added to the *kuku.*

EGGPLANT KUKU
(*Kukuye Bademjan*)

2 small eggplants
½ cup cooking oil
6 eggs, well beaten
1 tablespoon flour
½ teaspoon each salt, pepper, cloves, or saffron

(Serves 4 to 5)

Peel and dice eggplants and sauté them in half the cooking oil until soft and well browned. Mash thoroughly and add to beaten eggs. Stir in flour and spices. Heat remaining oil in an 8-inch frying pan, pour in egg mixture, and cook as for Vegetable *Kuku* above. Serve hot with bread and herbs or salad.

FISH KUKU
(*Kukuye Mahi*)

This is made in the same way as Vegetable *Kuku,* except that 1 small onion, chopped and fried, a pinch of cloves, and 2 cups fried flaked white fish, mashed, are substituted for the minced vegetables.

POTATO KUKU
(Kukuye Alu)

    1 pound potatoes
    1 small onion, grated
    6 eggs, well beaten
    1 tablespoon flour
    ½ teaspoon each salt, pepper, and curry powder
    1 tablespoon seedless white raisins
    2 tablespoons chopped parsley, sweet basil, or coriander
    ½ cup cooking oil

(Serves 4)

Peel and cook potatoes until soft. Mash well and mix with grated onion. Stir in eggs, flour, seasonings, raisins, and chopped parsley or basil. Heat oil in an 8-inch frying pan, pour in egg mixture, and cook as for Vegetable *Kuku*. Serve hot with bread, if desired.

NOTE: Cooked mashed pumpkin or beans may be substituted for the potatoes.

EGG KUKU
(Khagineh)

This *kuku*, similar to an American omelet, should be quickly made and served straight from the oven. It makes a delicious luncheon dish.

    6 eggs, well beaten
    1 tablespoon flour
    ½ cup salad oil

(Serves 4 to 5)

Combine eggs and flour and beat well. Heat oil until very hot in a frying pan, pour in egg mixture, and cook as for Vegetable *Kuku*. Serve hot, sprinkled with confectioners' sugar or honey. This *kuku* is usually turned out onto a plate lined with thin toast.

✐ Boranis
(Persian Salads)

In Persian cuisine *boranis* take the place of the American tossed salad or vegetables marinated in French dressing. Frequently they are served with bread as a simple meal, but more often as the salad course to a complete meal. I have found them very popular among my American friends. They are based on yogurt and different vegetables, and are served with *polous, kababs,* meat balls, soups, breads, and liquors.

SPINACH BORANI
(Borani Esfanaj)

1 pound fresh spinach
1 small onion, minced
½ tablespoon oil
2 cups yogurt
3 cloves garlic, minced
1 teaspoon powdered mint
2 tablespoons crushed toasted walnut meats
Salt and pepper to taste

(Serves 3 to 4)

Wash and chop spinach coarsely. Mix with the minced onion. Cook it with its own moisture in a frying pan over low heat, tossing frequently, until all water is evaporated. Add the oil and sauté about 3 minutes. Turn spinach into a salad bowl and mix lightly with the yogurt and garlic. Sprinkle with mint, walnuts and salt and pepper to taste.

EGGPLANT BORANI
(Borani Bademjan)

In this borani eggplant is substituted for the spinach. There are two ways of making it. The first is to peel and slice a large eggplant. Sprinkle slices with salt and stack them in a pile to remove the bitter juice. Then wash slices, dry, and fry them in good oil until browned on both sides. Add 2 tablespoons hot water, cover partially, and cook for about 10 minutes. When eggplant is tender and the water has cooked away, mash it with yogurt, salt, pepper, and minced garlic. Serve with *kababs*, *polous* and other foods, or as a snack with beverages, or with bread as a main dish.

The second method is as follows: Make a slit about 2 inches deep in the bottom of a large eggplant, put it in a baking dish and bake in a preheated 350° oven for about 45 minutes, or until tender. Then peel and mash eggplant, mix it with the yogurt, salt, pepper, and minced garlic. Coarsely chopped walnuts are frequently added. Small fried meat balls are added instead of walnuts when served with alcoholic beverages.

BEET BORANI

Cooked fresh or canned beets may be used. Chop or grate the beets and combine with yogurt, salt, pepper and powdered mint. This is one of the salads served during the winter months.

CUCUMBER BORANI
(Mastva Khiar)

(Serves 4 to 5)

This salad is the most popular of any in Persia. Grated cucumbers may simply be mixed with yogurt and seasoned with minced onion and salt and pepper, or a more elaborate concoction may be made:

Peel and grate 1 large or 2 small cucumbers and mix well with 1 or 2 cups yogurt. Add 4 tablespoons white raisins, ¼ cup chopped walnuts, 1 small onion, minced, salt, pepper, and powdered mint. Serve cold.

Another recipe adds to the cucumber and yogurt mixture, fresh or dried marjoram, sweet basil and mint, small white raisins, a few chopped dates, minced onion, chopped walnuts, and 1 or 2 chopped hard-cooked eggs. All the variations of *mastva khiar* are served with *polous, kababs,* stews, and with some soups. They are most refreshing in hot weather.

✒ Desserts

If you wish to be looked upon as sweet as halvaye-shekar,
Sow the seed of love in hearts as does halvaye-shekar.

RICE PUDDING
(Shir Berenj)

This is one of the most nutritious, delicious, and easiest to make of popular Persian desserts. Its heritage goes back to unknown times when Persians discovered that rice and milk cook to a delectable pudding. Ages ago it was served even to children as porridge for breakfast. Bos-hac says:

Oh, how delicious is a bowl of Shir Berenj in early morning
When your nurse rouses you from the bed!

According to legend, *shir berenj* was originally the food of angels, first made in heaven. When the prophet Mohammed ascended to the seventh floor of Heaven to meet God, he was served this dish.

During the religious nights of the fasting month, Ramadan, this dish is mandatory for the evening breakfast after sunset when the faithful Moslems break their fast, and also served at the feasts of Nazr. It is a favorite dessert of the rich and a nourishing main meal for the poor. It is not, however, customary to serve it at formal receptions.

2 cups (1 pound) rice
1 quart milk
2 cups water
1 cup sugar
½ cup rose water
1 teaspoon cardamom

(Serves 4)

Wash rice in several changes of hot water, then put it in a deep saucepan with the milk and water. Bring quickly to a boil, then reduce heat and cook over very low heat, stirring and folding occasionally to prevent rice from sticking to bottom, for 2 hours or until liquid has cooked away. Combine sugar, rose water, and cardamom and stir into the pudding. Cook, stirring, for 5 minutes. Pour into a serving dish and serve either hot or cold. Honey or grape molasses replaces the sugar when it is served cold.

YELLOW PUDDING
(Sholleh Zard)

*Maybe the candle of Sholleh Zard has entered through my door
That so brightened is my humble room!*

This is one of the most delicious puddings in all of Persian cuisine. It is enjoyed by young and old either as a main meal or for dessert. It does not seem ever to have been served for breakfast or at formal receptions, but both this dish and *shir berenj* are traditional for vow offerings (Nazr).

½ pound rice
6 cups cold water
½ teaspoon turmeric
3 cups hot water
2 tablespoons butter or shortening
1 cup rose water
2 cups sugar
½ teaspoon prepared saffron (see Index)
½ teaspoon each cardamom and cinnamon
¼ cup blanched shredded almonds

(Serves 6)

Wash rice in several changes of water. Bring the cold water to a boil. Add rice and turmeric, stir well, then simmer, covered, for about 30 minutes, or until most of the water has boiled away and rice is puffed and tender. Stir rice with a large perforated spoon while gradually adding the hot water. Add shortening and continue to cook the rice for about 2 hours, stirring occasionally. Then add rose water mixed with sugar and stir again until well blended. Stir in prepared saffron and cardamom, and cook, stirring, for about 10 minutes longer. Stir in nuts. Pour into a serving dish and sprinkle with cinnamon, making crisscross lines over the surface. Serve hot or cold. It will keep in refrigerator for a week.

HALVA

These are favorite dishes which have delighted Persians for many ages. There are many variations: some are made especially for religious occasions, some for their nutritive values and some simply for their deliciousness. But all are delicate and delectable desserts.

SUGAR HALVA
(Halvaye Shekar)

This may be called the grandfather of all *halvas*, since it is the oldest. For ages it has been served as a vow offering for the health of a child, and for mourners' dinners. The people in southern Persia still serve this *halva* for breakfast.

 1 pound coarse wheat flour
 1 pound (2 cups) hot cooking oil
 1 pound sugar
 ½ cup rose water or water
 1 teaspoon prepared saffron (see Index)
 1 teaspoon cardamom

(Serves 4 to 5)

Roast the flour in a large saucepan over low heat, stirring constantly, until it turns yellow. Add oil gradually, stirring vigorously to mix it with the flour, and continue to cook until flour and oil mixture becomes light brown. Melt sugar in rose water or water and stir it gradually into the fried flour mixture. Continue to cook over low heat until the excess oil starts to rise to the surface. Add saffron and cardamom and cook for 5 minutes longer, stirring constantly. Remove pan from heat but continue to fold and stir for about 10 minutes. Return mixture to heat and stir for 5 minutes longer, or until excess oil covers the top. Remove oil with a spoon and set aside to use for another purpose. Put *halva* in a deep serving bowl and press it with the back of a large tablespoon against the sides to make a thick layer inside the bowl, formed into the shape of rose leaves. Serve hot or cold.

DATE HALVA
(*Halvaye Khorma*)

Among the oldest and most delicious *halvas*, this one made of dates is known to every Persian, yet it is customarily served only as a food offering to the poor at funeral ceremonies and other religious occasions in the holy days of the months of Ramadan and Muharram. It is never served at any happy occasion.

It is made in the same way as the sugar *halva* except that 1 pound soft fresh dates, stoned and mashed, are used in place of the sugar.

Toast the flour and stir in the oil. When golden brown, stir in ½ cup rose water or ¼ cup hot water, if rose water is not available. Add the dates and mix well on the fire. Add saffron and cardamom and proceed as for sugar *halva*.

HALVA OF FLOWERS

These exotic *halvas* are popular at dinner parties and other gay social events. They are made either with the aromatic and tender flower petal of small five-petal white or yellow roses, jasmine, or orange or quince blossoms or with water extracted from these flowers. The one made with white roses, known as *nastaran*, is perhaps the simplest of all to make.

WHITE HALVA
(*Halvaye Safid*)

The surface of a plate of Halvaye Safid
Is so freshly beautiful that it wins the stake on beauty
From the spring flower garden.

½ cup vegetable oil

1 pound rice flour

1 pound confectioners' sugar

1 cup rose water or water

2 cups water

½ pound fresh small white rose petals (*nastaran*, see Index)

1 teaspoon cardamom

¼ cup chopped pistachios or blanched almonds

In a large saucepan melt oil, stir in rice flour, and fry until the mixture turns to a light cream color—not brown. Dissolve sugar in the flower water, add to the frying flour and mix thoroughly. Bring the 2 cups water to a boil, add the rose petals and simmer for 4 to 5 minutes. Drain, rinse in cool water, and mince the petals. Stir petals and cardamom into the flour mixture and cook, stirring, for about 15 minutes. Remove pan from heat and continue to fold and stir for 10 minutes. Return mixture to heat and stir for 5 minutes longer, or until excess oil covers the top. Remove oil with a spoon and set aside for another use. Put *halva* into a deep serving bowl and press it with the back of a tablespoon against the sides to make a thick layer inside the bowl in the shape of rose leaves. Sprinkle with the nuts.

NOTE: If yellow *halva* is preferred, add ½ teaspoon saffron along with the cardamom.

HALVAYE GOL

Delicate and delicious are the *halvas* made of jasmine, orange or quince blossoms, or small yellow roses.

What a fragrance! The bowl of Halvaye Gol!
With delicate sweet scent

These *halvas* are made in exactly the same way as *halvaye safid*. Sometimes wheat starch is substituted for the rice flour. In this case mix 1 pound starch with about 1 cup cold water until mixture looks like milk. Pour into a saucepan and bring to a boil. When it starts to thicken, add the oil and stir vigorously. Fry until starch turns creamy in color. Then add sugar melted with the flower water, the minced petals, and the cardamom and continue as for other *halvas*. Sprinkle with crushed pistachios or chopped blanched almonds. Serve hot or cold.

LITTLE COLORED HALVA
(*Rangenak*)

1¼ pounds fresh dates
4 ounces (½ cup) shelled walnuts
8 ounces wheat flour
8 ounces buckwheat flour
¾ cup vegetable oil
½ cup sugar
3 tablespoons confectioners' sugar
2 teaspoons each cardamom, cinnamon, nutmeg, and clove

Stone dates. Toast the walnut meats and chop coarsely. Knead the dates with the hands until soft and blended, then knead in the nuts. Sprinkle a cooky sheet generously with cinnamon. Place the date dough in the center of the sheet and press it against the bottom and edges to make an even layer about 1 inch thick.

Combine the wheat flour and buckwheat flour and toast it in a skillet, stirring constantly until it turns creamy in color. In a small saucepan heat the oil and stir it gradually into the flour mixture. Keep stirring and folding over low heat until mixture is smooth and golden brown and the excess oil rises to the surface. Combine sugars and half the spices and stir into the flour mixture. Continue cooking and stirring until everything is as soft as a cake frosting. Pour the frosting mixture quickly over the date dough. This second layer should be about ⅓ inch thick and should cover the date dough. Let cool for 30 minutes, then sprinkle evenly first with confectioners' sugar and then with the remaining spices. With a sharp, oiled knife, cut the dough into 1-inch squares and leave on the sheet until completely cool.

MILK HALVA
(Halvaye Shir)

This *halva* is frequently distributed to the poor during the month of Ramadan.

½ cup vegetable oil
4 ounces rice flour
1 quart milk
4 tablespoons rose water
½ cup sugar
1 teaspoon cardamom
½ cup confectioners' sugar
½ teaspoon prepared saffron (optional)
⅓ cup chopped pistachios or blanched almonds

In a deep pot heat the oil. Stir in flour and fry slightly. Gradually stir in milk and continue to stir until mixture is smooth. Add rose water, sugar, and cardamom and cook, stirring, until thick. Add confectioners' sugar and saffron if desired and stir until sugar is dissolved. Pour into a large flat dish or onto a shallow cooky sheet moistened with water, and sprinkle with nuts. Cool, then cut into large oblong pieces. The *halva* may be poured into individual serving bowls and sprinkled with nuts.

✑ Pastries and Confections

Being so delicate and graceful, Lady Qotaab wears
Always a fine blouse of dough.
Since the Maiden-Qotaab has her head opened
A veil of fine dough is made for her.

A nation as old as Persia has necessarily influenced the culture of its surrounding countries. This is true of the culinary art as well as other crafts, and is particularly noticeable in the confection category where, even today, many sweet delicacies are exported in large quantities to her neighboring nations. Among them are *baglava, kotab,* and *pashmak* which are indigenous to Yazd in eastern Iran; *kolucheh* (a patty of rice) from Hamadan in west central Iran; *gazz* from Isfahan, central Iran; *komach* from Shiraz, southwest central Iran, and *basloq* from Kerman in the southeast.

PERSIAN PIE
(*Baglava*)

So much overwhelmed am I today by Baglava
That it should not befit me to care for
The shadowy delight of Ardeh-Khorma

During the centuries all the neighboring countries of Persia have copied *baglava*, but none of the adaptations is as delicate

or delicious as that made by Persian women. Traditionally
it is served for Nowrooze and other happy occasions.

   1 pound almonds
   Jasmine, orange or pussy-willow blossoms, or vanilla bean
   1 pound cube sugar
   1 pound cake flour
   1½ cups hot vegetable oil
   7 tablespoons milk
   2 eggs, well beaten
   About ½ cup water
   1 cup sugar
   ½ cup hot water

Blanch the almonds about twenty days before making the
baglava, dry them well, and perfume them by putting them
in a deep jar or bowl fitted with a tight cover and filling the
jar with flower blossoms (a vanilla bean may be used in place
of the flowers to perfume the almonds). Cover closely and add
flowers daily for ten to twelve days, stirring almonds each time.
When well perfumed, remove flowers and keep the almonds
tightly covered, ready for use.

When ready to make the *baglava,* pound the almonds with
the cube sugar in a mortar. If the mortar is not large enough
to hold both almonds and sugar, pound a little at a time until
all almonds and sugar are pounded and mixed together. Sieve
the mixture through a large-holed sieve.

Sift the flour into a bowl. Combine 4 tablespoons of the
shortening with the milk and eggs and stir into the flour along
with enough water to make a dough. Knead dough until
smooth and glossy. Cover with a towel and let it rest in a warm
place for 30 minutes. Then turn onto a floured board and knead
again thoroughly.

Take part of the dough, about the size of a very small orange, and roll it out on a lightly floured board into a round sheet about 20 inches in diameter, and as thin as paper. Cut the circle into four equal parts, making four triangles. Place the triangles, one at a time, on a clean wooden board and sprinkle with the almonds and sugar mixture. Then roll into a cylinder about 1½ inches thick and 6 to 7 inches long, beginning at the acute angle and rolling to the curved edge. Place the cylinder in a baking dish about 1½ inches deep and 6 inches wide, letting the cylinder overhang on both sides of the dish. Continue rolling the triangles of dough and arranging them in pans, packing them as closely as sardines in a can. When pans are full, cut off surplus ends overhanging the pans with an oiled knife, and cut the cylinders into 1½-inch squares. Sprinkle lightly with remaining hot oil, letting it flow through the cuts and over the surface by moving and swirling the dish from side to side. Bake in a preheated 375° oven for about 30 minutes, or until top of the *baglava* becomes a reddish brown.

While the *baglava* is baking, combine sugar and water and cook over high heat until syrup spins a long thread. When *baglava* is done, remove from oven and quickly pour the thick syrup over it. Swirl the pan so that all surfaces will be coated with the syrup. Cool. Then carefully remove the squares and store in a tightly closed container.

Chopped pistachios may be used in place of the almonds.

ALMOND SQUARES
(*Lauze Badam*)

This is another ancient but highly favored sweetmeat for special occasions. The making of these almond squares is similar to the making of fondant candy, which is popular in America at Christmas time.

½ pound cube sugar

1 pound blanched almonds perfumed with flowers or vanilla (see *baglava*)

2 cups sugar

⅔ cup hot water

Pound the cube sugar and almonds in a mortar with a pestle until coarsely crushed in the same way as for *baglava*. Sieve and reserve ⅓ cup of the finest part. Combine the sugar and water and cook over high heat until the syrup spins a long thread. Remove from heat and stir until cool enough to handle. Add the almond-sugar mixture and knead to make a white dough. Quickly form dough into a ball. Then sprinkle a thin layer of the reserved almonds and sugar on a flat china or glass dish. Place ball of dough in center and, with palms of the hands or a rolling pin, flatten dough until it is 1 inch thick, gradually sprinkling over it the remaining almonds and sugar to prevent the dough from sticking to the rolling pin or hands. Let it set for 3 hours, then cut it into 1½-inch squares with an oiled knife.

If the almonds are not scented with flowers or vanilla, sprinkle the dough with 1 teaspoon cardamom or vanilla when you are flattening it on the plate. About ½ teaspoon saffron may also be added to the dough to make it yellow; then it is called "yellow *lauze*." Place the squares in a tightly closed box or tin and store in a cool, dry place.

SHIRAZI LAUZE

Many elaborate variations of almond squares are called *shirazi lauze* because the ladies of that city are famous for making the best of them. A few typical varieties follow:

MULBERRY LAUZE
(*Toot*)

This is actually the same as almond *lauze*, except that the shape is changed. When the dough is ready to be flattened, divide it into small pieces as large as a mulberry and shape each piece into the facsimile of a mulberry. Roll in granulated sugar and insert a lengthwise sliver of a pistachio in the bottom of each to represent the stem.

COCONUT SQUARES
(*Lauze Narjeel*)

This is a favorite sweetmeat at Nowrooze and other special occasions. It must be very white and fine-grained and is easy to make.

Peel and grate 1 pound coconut and spread on a clean towel. Combine 1 pound sugar with 1 cup hot water, bring to a boil and boil until it spins a long thread. Remove from heat. Add all but about 3 tablespoons of the shredded coconut and blend and knead with the fingers until the dough is smooth and white. Continue as for almond squares, sprinkling the dough with the remaining coconut instead of almonds. If dough is sticky, sprinkle with confectioners' sugar.

HONEY SQUARES
(*Lauze Asali*)

Pound 1 pound blanched almonds, then knead with enough honey to make a thick paste. Flatten the paste on a dish to a thickness of about 1 inch. Boil 1 pound sugar (2 cups) with ⅔ cup water until it spins a long thread. Beat until white and creamy and pour over the paste. Sprinkle generously with 2 ounces crushed pistachios mixed with ½ teaspoon cardamom. Press slightly with a rolling pin or the palms of the hands and, when still warm, cut into squares.

PATTY OF HONEY
(Sahoone Asali)

This elaborate confection ranks in popularity with *baglava* and *lauze*. It is customary to serve it at New Year's and at wedding and birthday celebrations. Frequently a large dish of *sahoone asali* is sent by an employee to his employer or to a dear friend as a token of great esteem.

½ pound shelled almonds
1 cup sugar
⅓ cup hot water
½ cup honey
½ cup good cooking oil
½ teaspoon prepared saffron (see Index) or cardamom and cloves
Crushed pistachios and finely chopped coconut, mixed

Blanch and sliver the almonds lengthwise. Combine sugar and water in a saucepan, bring to a boil, and boil over high heat until syrup spins a long thread. Add honey and almonds and let the syrup cook for 10 minutes, stirring constantly. When it begins to turn amber in color, stir in the oil and continue to stir until the almond shreds look brown and a little of the syrup becomes very brittle when dropped into cold water. Stir in the saffron or cardamom and cloves.

Now reduce heat to very low and work quickly. Oil two cooky trays. Drop the candy on the trays from a long-handled spoon into rounds about 1 inch in diameter, keeping each round about an inch away from the other. Someone else must stand beside the trays with a knife, helping to shape the syrup into rounds as soon as it is dropped from the spoon and is still hot and soft. It becomes hard and brittle almost at once. Quickly sprinkle each round with mixed nuts. Keep the syrup over low heat until it is all dropped onto the trays. Let stand for 30 minutes, then remove with a spatula. If they stick to the tray, try slightly warming the tray to soften the candies. Place candies one by one on absorbent paper to remove the oil, then arrange in a tin or box with paper under each patty to prevent it from sticking. Cover tightly and store in a cool, dry place.

RICE PATTY
(Kolucheh Berenj)

This small, delicate cooky is made only in Persian homes. The people of Hamadan (the capital of ancient Media, in western Persia) and Kermanshah, another old city in the west, are specialists in making it. The recipe I am giving here is a Shirazian variation which was made by my grandmothers and mother before me. It is usually served with another sweetmeat known as *Masqati* and is popular at sad as well as at happy occasions. Bos-hac admires these two confections:

> *To two moons I did liken Kolucheh and Masqati*
> *Yet be sure, their beauty is beyond such comparison*

    1 cup good shortening
    1 cup confectioners' sugar
    1 egg
    1 egg yolk
    3 cups (12 ounces) fine rice flour
    1 teaspoon cardamom
    Finely chopped pistachios

Melt shortening and pour into a mixing bowl. Beat vigorously with a large spoon until the shortening becomes creamy and fluffy. Gradually stir in sugar and beat until mixture is fluffy. Beat egg and yolk thoroughly and stir into the sugar mixture. Gradually stir in flour and cardamom and knead with fingers to make a smooth, soft dough. Let dough stand at room temperature for about 1 hour, then shape into balls the size of large hazelnuts. Place balls on a cooky sheet about ½ inch apart and, with the edge of a thimble, make two or three half circles on each for decoration. Sprinkle with chopped nuts and bake in a preheated 375° oven for 12 to 15 minutes, or until the bottom of each cooky is slightly brown. Remove from oven, let cool for 5 minutes, then store in a tightly covered box in a dry place.

MASQATI

6 pounds sugar
1 pound cornstarch
About 6 cups water
1 cup warm cooking oil
½ pound finely crushed almonds
2 teaspoons cardamom
Finely ground pistachio nuts

Combine sugar and cornstarch with enough water to make a mixture as thin as milk. Boil over medium heat, stirring constantly, until sugar is dissolved. Add oil. Continue to boil, stirring until the bubbles cover the surface like a thick blanket. Remove from fire and add almonds and cardamom. Mix and pour into a deep baking dish to a thickness of 1½ inches. Sprinkle generously with finely ground, sieved pistachios. Let stand for about 1 hour, or until firm enough to cut. Cut into

1-inch squares and let set for 2 hours longer. Remove squares with a spatula and store in a tightly covered dish in a cool, dry place.

ZOLOBIYA

Of sweet Zolo-biya chain I hung a necklace around her neck.
From its delicious loops I made a ring on her ears.

Here is another confection which is as old as the story of *One Thousand and One Nights,* for the name is mentioned in many stories in the book. It is served only at informal home parties and nightly gatherings during the month of Ramadan. It is also a favorite present to the poor during this month.

For making this confection, the Persians have always used a mineral salt which is gathered and dried on the shores of the Persian Gulf. It is white and very fluffy and is called *kafe darya,* meaning sea foam. Bicarbonate of soda is an appropriate substitute for it.

> 4 ounces (½ cup) yogurt
> 1 pound wheat starch or cornstarch
> 1 tablespoon good oil
> 1 teaspoon soda
> 1 pound, 12 ounces (3½ cups) sugar
> 2 cups hot water
> 2 tablespoons honey
> Shortening or oil for deep frying

Gradually combine yogurt and starch, add oil and soda and stir well, making a smooth dough, thin enough to flow through a large funnel. Cover and let rise for 1 hour. Meanwhile combine sugar and water and boil over high heat until the syrup spins a thread. Stir in honey and boil for 3 minutes longer. Remove from heat and keep warm.

Heat shortening or oil to a depth of 1 inch in a large frying pan. Pour the batter into the hot oil through a large funnel, blocking half the hole with the middle finger and moving the funnel in a circle to form several circles twisted together and as large as three inches in diameter. Cook the circles until golden, dip in the warm syrup, and place in a sieve or on a perforated tray placed over a cooky sheet to drain. Cool and store in a tightly covered container.

LITTLE PUFFS
(Pofak)

This delicate candy is served mostly with cocktails.

3 egg whites
1 cup confectioners' sugar
1 tablespoon lemon juice
½ teaspoon citric acid
½ teaspoon cardamom

Beat egg whites until stiff but not dry. Gradually beat in the sugar and continue beating, adding drop by drop the lemon juice mixed with the citric acid, until the meringue is very thick and glossy. Beat in the cardamom.

Cut strips of white paper 3 inches wide and about 18 inches long. Place each strip on a strip of cardboard cut the same size as the paper. Hold paper and cardboard together firmly with the left hand to prevent paper from slipping, and with the right hand dip up a little of the meringue on the back of a teaspoon and place it on the right edge of the paper, pressing spoon downward in such a way that the meringue forms a tiny half moon on the edge of the paper. Make another one about ¼ inch away from the first and continue until right edge of paper is full. Repeat all along the left edge of paper. Hang the strips on a clothesline to dry at room temperature. Needless to say, the room in which these little meringues are to dry must be free from excess humidity, which Americans may find difficult at certain times of the year! Perhaps the better solution is to put the meringues in an oven preheated to 250°, then turn off the heat and let the meringues dry in the warm oven or hang them in a sunny room. When completely dry they will come off the paper at a touch. Store in a tightly closed box, and they will last for months.

CHERRY CANDY
(*Noqle Alu Balu*)

This is another delicate candy served with cocktails and at private parties. The ingredients and preparation of the meringue are exactly the same as for making *pofak*. When the meringue is thick, wash and dry 2 pounds fresh sour cherries with stems. Then take each one by the stem and dip it into the meringue to coat the cherry completely. Place coated cherries on a cooky sheet lined with plain white paper and put in a warm place to dry. (A warming oven is an excellent place, or a radiator in a warm, dry room.)

WINDOW BREAD
(*Nane Penjereh*)

8 eggs
1¾ cups milk
1¾ cups flour
1 teaspoon cardamom
Shortening or oil for deep frying

Beat eggs until thick and light in color. Stir in milk and gradually stir in flour and finally the cardamom. Beat well.

The batter should be the consistency of heavy cream and free from lumps. Heat shortening in a small deep saucepan to 375°. Heat a brass or aluminum rosette iron in the hot oil, shake off excess oil, and dip iron quickly into the batter, being careful not to let the batter cover more than ⅔ the depth of the iron. Lower iron into the hot shortening and, as soon as the batter sets and begins to expand, shake the iron to allow the rosette to slip off. Fry until a light golden brown. Place upside down on absorbent paper to drain. Heat mold again in the oil for a second and continue, stirring batter frequently, until all batter is used. Sprinkle generously with confectioners' sugar and store in a tightly covered container in a cool, dry place. If the batter sticks to the iron, the oil is too hot.

ELEPHANT-EAR COOKIES
(Nane Goosh Feel)

3 egg yolks
1 egg white
¼ cup rose water or water
½ cup milk
½ teaspoon cardamom
About 14 ounces (about 3½ cups) sifted flour
Shortening or good oil for deep frying

Beat egg yolks and white and combine with the rose water, milk, and cardamom. Gradually stir in enough flour to make a soft dough, turn dough out on a lightly floured board, and knead until firm, smooth, and glossy. Cover and let stand for 2 hours. Divide into balls the size of small walnuts. Then with a rolling pin roll each ball out as thin as paper 3 inches in diameter and cut into rounds. With the fingers gather one side of the round and press dough together into a tiny handle ⅓ inch in length and thickness. The remainder of the circle should flare out like an elephant's ear. The round may be cut in half, if desired, and the diameter edge of each half circle gathered together so that the cooky resembles a Chinese fan. Place the cookies on a cooky sheet and keep them covered with a towel to prevent them from drying. When all the dough is fashioned into "fans" or "ears," heat oil to a depth of about 1 inch in a shallow frying pan to 375°. Fry the cookies a few at a time in the hot oil for about 30 seconds on one side, then turn and fry the other. They should not be allowed to brown much. Remove and drain on absorbent paper. While still warm, sprinkle generously with confectioners' sugar. Store in a tightly closed container in a dry place.

DAHLIA COOKIES
(Gol Kaukab)

3 eggs
½ cup milk
¼ cup rose water or water
½ teaspoon cardamom
About 14 ounces (about 3½ cups) sifted flour
Shortening or oil for deep frying
1 egg yolk

Beat whole eggs until well blended and combine with milk, rose water, and cardamom. Gradually stir in flour to make a soft dough. Turn dough out onto a lightly floured board and knead until firm, smooth, and glossy. Cover and let stand for 2 hours. Divide dough into balls the size of a small apple. Roll out each ball on the floured board until it is as thin as paper and cut into 3-inch rounds. When all the dough has been cut into rounds, place one round on a cooky sheet. Beat the egg yolk slightly with a fork and drip one drop in the center of the round. Place another round over it and drip a drop of yolk over this second one. Repeat until there are 6 rounds, piled one on top of the other. Press the center of pile firmly with the finger against the bottom of the cooky sheet. Then with a small, sharp knife cut 6 slits, equally spaced, through the cooky at right angles to the center, being careful not to cut through the center.

Heat shortening in a saucepan to 375°. Insert a small stick or pencil into the center of one of the cookies and carefully lift up and separate the sections of dough, which radiate from the center like the petals of a flower. Dip the "flower" by the stick into the hot oil. Fry, but do not brown, turning the stick constantly so that the hot shortening can flow between the petals. Remove stick and with a large, perforated spoon or sugar tongs remove the cooky carefully to drain on absorbent paper. While warm, sprinkle generously with confectioners' sugar. This recipe makes 18 very beautiful and delicious "dahlias." Store in a tightly closed container in a dry place.

TURNOVER COOKIES
(Kotab)

This cooky is still as dear to the Persians as it was to Bos-hac 700 years ago. The people of Yezd, an ancient city in Eastern Persia, are specialists in making them. They pack them in small tin boxes and send them to markets all through Persia and to neighboring countries.

The ingredients for these cookies are exactly the same for Elephant Ears (see Index).

After the dough is made, cover and keep it in a warm place for about 2 hours. Then turn dough out on a lightly floured board and knead well. Divide dough into portions the size of apples. Roll out each portion on the floured board until it is as thin as a cabbage leaf, and cut it into rounds 3½ inches in diameter. Mix together equal parts of finely pounded almonds, pistachios or hazelnuts, and sugar. Cinnamon, cardamom, or cloves may also be added. Place 1 tablespoon of the mixture over half of each round. Brush edge with lightly beaten egg yolk and fold in half. Press edges together firmly, then gather the diameter edge of each cooky together with the fingers to shape each cooky like a half moon. Roll the gathered edge about ¼ inch think and score with a sharp knife. Fry cookies in deep shortening, heated to 375°, until lightly browned. Drain on absorbent paper and sprinkle generously with confectioners' sugar. Store in a tightly closed container in a dry place.

✍ Preserves and Beverages

Be always loyal to the friend who,
Though sour in form, is sweet in meaning

Preserves
(Moraba)

For countless generations the Persians have preserved all manner of vegetables, fruits, and flower petals, first in honey or molasses, and later in sugar to serve as dessert or at the breakfast table. Cardamom seeds are the favorite flavoring for all preserves. They should be crushed fairly finely in a small mortar with a pestle and added to the preserve 2 to 3 minutes before it is to be removed from the heat.

CHERRY PRESERVE
(Moraba Alu Balu)

1 pound sugar
1 cup water
1 pound pitted sour black cherries
1 teaspoon crushed cardamom

Combine sugar and water in a saucepan, bring to a boil, and boil rapidly until syrup spins a thread. Add cherries to the boiling syrup and boil rapidly until the cherries look transparent. Add the cardamom and boil for 2 to 3 minutes longer. Remove cherries from syrup with a perforated spoon and put them in a wide-mouthed jar. Again boil syrup until it spins a long thread. Remove from heat, let cool for 5 minutes, then pour over the cherries. Leave uncovered for 2 days in a cool place. Then seal with jar lid and store at room temperature.

One pound apricots or peaches may be substituted for the cherries, but in these preserves ¼ cup shelled and crushed pistachios are usually added along with the cardamom.

APPLE PRESERVE
(*Morabaye Sib*)

Apple, quince, and citron are the oldest known preserves in Persian cuisine. Ginger, cloves, mace, and nutmeg were used as flavorings as well as the ubiquitous cardamom. Today these spices are still used in certain parts of the country. In Jahrum, an ancient city in southern Persia, the people make a delicious date preserve flavored with ginger. It would be impossible to give all the recipes here, but certainly you may substitute other spices for the cardamom if you wish.

    1 pound large sour apples
    2 cups cold water
    2 tablespoons white vinegar
    1 pound (2 cups) sugar
    1½ cups hot water
    1 tablespoon lemon juice
    ¾ cup shelled almonds and pistachios, mixed
    ½ teaspoon cardamom

The apples are kept whole. Peel them, but do not remove cores or stems. Drop them immediately into the cold water mixed with the vinegar to prevent them from discoloring. Bring the sugar, hot water, and lemon juice to a boil. Add apples and boil rapidly until the syrup spins a thread and the apples are soft and transparent. Remove apples and put them in a wide-mouthed jar. Again cook syrup until it spins a long thread. Add nuts and spice and boil for 10 minutes longer. Pour syrup over the fruit and let stand, uncovered, for 2 days. Then seal and store in a cool, dry place.

ORANGE PRESERVE
(*Morabaye Narange*)

This is a beautiful preserve with a most delicious flavor.

3 large, thick-skinned oranges
2 pounds granulated sugar
2 cups water
½ tablespoon crushed cardamom seeds

Shave a thin layer of the skin off the oranges. A thin yellow layer must remain. Put the oranges into a bowl filled with cold water for 3 days, changing the water 4 times each day. After 3 days, put the oranges in a saucepan with fresh water and bring to a boil. Drain, cover with fresh water, and bring to a boil again. Repeat this process twice more and drain. Combine sugar and water, bring to a boil, and boil until syrup spins a very long, thick thread. Meanwhile make a few shallow slits in the sides of each orange with a sharp-pointed knife. As soon as the syrup is thick, add the oranges and cook until the oranges are transparent, turning them frequently and gently. Pour oranges and syrup into a china bowl and let stand for 24 hours. Drain oranges and return the syrup to the heat. Add the cardamom, bring syrup to a boil, and boil rapidly for 10 minutes. Transfer oranges to a wide-mouthed jar. Pour hot syrup over the oranges, seal tightly, and store in a cool, dry place. The oranges look like whole fresh ones.

WALNUT PRESERVE
(Morabaye Gerdu)

This is a unique preserve made best by the elder citizens of Shiraz. There they make a social production of the making of the preserve. At least three people help to peel the green walnuts, each person in turn cutting only one round of peel from each walnut as fast as possible and passing it along to the next person, who uses a clean knife to remove the second round of peel. The knives are washed in between each round.

    2 tablespoons white vinegar
    2 pounds green walnuts (the first and second skins must
        be still tender and green)
    4 heaping tablespoons slaked lime
    1 pound cube sugar
    1 cup hot water
    4 tablespoons white vinegar
    ½ teaspoon crushed cardamom seeds

Fill a large bowl with cold water and add the 2 tablespoons of vinegar. With a sharp knife remove a thin layer of peel from a walnut and continue removing thin layers until all the walnuts are peeled, washing the knife after each layer is removed. Each peeled walnut is dropped immediately into the bowl of acidulated water to preserve the color. Then in a large crock mix the slaked lime with 4 quarts of water. Stir thoroughly and let stand until a layer of powder forms in the bottom of the crock. Drain the walnuts and pour the lime-water over them, being careful not to include the sediment in the bottom of the crock, and let the walnuts soak in the lime-water for 6 hours. Drain and rinse the walnuts in fresh cold water many times until no trace of lime remains. Cover with fresh water and let stand for 6 hours longer.

Combine sugar and hot water and bring to a boil. Add the 4 tablespoons vinegar and boil rapidly until the syrup spins a thread. Drain and add walnuts and boil until the walnut meat is soft and transparent. They should be white, not dark in color. Add the cardamom and boil for 2 to 3 minutes longer. Cool, then pack into clean jars, seal, and store. They look beautiful and taste delicious.

CARROT PRESERVE
(*Morabaye Havij*)

The native carrot of Persia is a tender, juicy, sweet variety, pale yellow in color. It is made into a nutritious preserve during the winter months when fruits are not available.

 2 pounds young carrots
 2 tablespoons slaked lime
 1 pound sugar
 1 cup hot water
 ½ teaspoon cardamom seeds
 3 ounces shelled pistachios or almonds

Scrape carrots and cut them into thin rounds. Remove the hard center from each piece to form rings. Cover with lime-water made by mixing the slaked lime with 4 quarts cold water (see preceding recipe) and let stand for 12 hours. Rinse thoroughly, cover with fresh water, and let stand for 12 hours. Rinse thoroughly and drain.

Combine sugar and water, bring to a boil, and boil rapidly

until syrup spins a long thread. Add carrots and boil until carrots are tender and transparent. Add cardamom and nuts and boil for 3 minutes longer. Cool and pack in tightly closed jars and store in a cool place.

FLOWER PRESERVE
(Gol Moraba)

The Persian women have always had an extraordinary fondness for and appreciation of flowers. From ancient times they have devised many dishes of sweets and preserves from perfumed flower petals. One made of orange blossoms by the natives of Hamadan and Kermanshah is sold in the markets, but it is never quite as good as the homemade variety, which is a fine, white, tender, and fragrant preserve.

⅓ pound dried white orange blossoms, or 1 pound fresh
1 pound sugar
1 cup hot water
½ teaspoon crushed cardamom
½ cup crushed pistachios or almonds

Pour 2 cups fresh cold water over the petals and let them stand for 1 hour. Drain, cover with fresh water, and bring slowly to a boil. Boil for 1 to 2 minutes, drain, and rinse the petals in ice water. Drain again thoroughly.

Make a thick, heavy syrup of the sugar and hot water, boiling until it spins a long thread. Add the cardamom and nuts and boil for 5 minutes. Add the petals and boil for 1 minute longer. Remove from heat and pour into preserving jar. Cool, cover tightly, and store in a cool, dry place. This preserve does not keep as long as other preserves.

Preserves of quince blossoms, small yellow 5-petal roses, and jasmine are made in the same way. Only the jasmine petals do not need boiling. Simply cover them in cold fresh water for 2 hours, rinse and drain thoroughly, and add to the syrup. The syrup for these preserves must be very thick.

WATERMELON PRESERVE

1 pound watermelon rind
4 heaping tablespoons slaked lime
1 pound sugar
1 cup hot water
1 teaspoon crushed cardamom seeds

Remove the thin green part from the rind and cut rind into small squares about ½ inch thick. Add the lime to 4 quarts cold water, stir, and let stand until a thin layer of white sediment falls to the bottom of the crock (always use a china or crockery bowl for limewater). Pour the limewater over the rind, being careful not to include the sediment from the bottom, and put in the refrigerator to chill for 48 hours. Drain and rinse thoroughly. Cover watermelon rind with fresh cold water and let stand for 6 hours. Change water twice more, letting rind soak for 6 hours each time, or a total of 18 hours. Rinse thoroughly, put pieces in a saucepan, cover with fresh water, and bring to a boil. Drain, cover with cold water, bring to a boil again, and boil until the rind is transparent. Drain, rinse, and drain again.

Boil the sugar with the water until it spins a thread. Add the rind and continue to boil until the rind is crisp and very transparent and the syrup is thick. Add cardamom and cook for 3 minutes longer. Pour into a china bowl and let stand for 12 hours. Return to saucepan and again boil until syrup is very thick, or for about 10 minutes. Pour into preserving jars, seal, and store in a cool place.

Pumpkin may be substituted for the watermelon. The hard, yellow peel must be removed before the pumpkin is diced.

PICKLES
(*Torshis*)

Pickles are essential to Persian food and always accompany the various polous, kababs, and fried meats. Even the poorest home in the country has a supply of pickles, for it is a general belief that pickles not only are appetizing and appetite-stimulating but are necessary to the functioning of the body chemistry. The acidity of the pickles helps to consume the oils and starches in the body and aids digestion by relieving the work of the stomach and liver. Therefore, in the course of ages, pickles of fruits, vegetables, and the peels of fruits have been devised, all based on strong cider or grape vinegar and a variety of spices, such as red and green pepper, cinnamon, cardamom, mace, nutmeg, turmeric, ginger, and coriander, as well as the many available seeds—fennel, anise, white poppy and mustard—and also garlic and tamarind.

PEACH PICKLES
(*Torshi Holu*)

1 tablespoon finely chopped dried ginger
4 cups grape vinegar
2 tablespoons coriander seed
1 whole bulb garlic
1 pound fresh or dried peaches
¼ pound dried tamarind (if available)
½ teaspoon red pepper
½ cup cubed sugar
1 teaspoon salt
1 teaspoon black pepper

Soak the ginger in 1 cup of the vinegar for 2 days. Soak the peaches also, if they are dried. Toast coriander seeds slightly. Peel and separate garlic cloves. Combine peaches with the ginger, coriander, garlic, and 3 cups of vinegar. Soak the tamarind in the remaining cup of vinegar and rub between the fingers until all the tamarind pulp is smoothly dissolved. Strain the liquid into the other ingredients. Add the red pepper mixed with the sugar, salt, and black pepper. Bring to a boil and boil for 5 minutes. If the pickle is too thick, add a little more vinegar.

One half pound of any or all of the following ingredients may be added to this pickle: dried chopped prunes, plums, apricots, cherries, apples, figs, or persimmons; fresh or dried limes; small unpeeled oranges or tangerines, chopped.

When the pickles are done, all the ingredients must be covered with vinegar. If sweet fruits are used, the sugar should be eliminated and the ginger should be doubled. Put pickles into a perserving jar and fill jar to overflowing with vinegar. Seal, but check every few days. If the vinegar is absorbed, open the jar and add more. These pickles are delicious with all sorts of rice and meat dishes.

PICKLED LIMES
(Torshi Limu)

This is one of the most popular pickles in Iran, and the women of Shiraz are renowned for making it superbly.

With a rough, clean stone or a fine grater scrub the skin of 20 large fresh limes until all the green is removed. They must look like small white balls. Roll the limes in salt until they are thickly coated and place them in the sun or a very warm room to dry. When well dried, brush off the salt and pack them in a preserving jar. Cover with white or distilled vinegar. Close tightly and keep at room temperature.

Dried limes may be kept in a covered jar and soaked in vinegar whenever they are needed. Lemon juice may be substituted for the vinegar. This *torshi* is best with *kababs, polous,* or *qa'meh.*

QUICK PICKLED LIMES

Split 20 large limes into 4 sections, leaving them intact at the bottom. Stuff each lime with salt and place one on top of another in a basket in the sun to dry for at least 20 days. Then store in a cool, dry place. When needed, remove the salt from as many limes as desired and pack them in a jar. Cover with red-wine vinegar, cover, and keep at room temperature for about 1 week before serving with any kind of meats and polous.

PERSIMMON PICKLE
(*Torshi Khramlu*)

2 pounds ripe persimmons, chopped
3 dried limes, chopped (*limu omani*)
1 tablespoon dry mustard
½ tablespoon red pepper
1 tablespoon black pepper
2 cups grape vinegar
1 tablespoon crushed cardamom seeds
1 tablespoon grated nutmeg
1 cup toasted coriander seeds
2 tablespoons sweet-fennel seeds
1 tablespoon anise seeds
2 teaspoons salt
1 tablespoon cinnamon
1 tablespoon crushed cloves
1 tablespoon toasted poppy seeds
2 whole bulbs garlic, peeled and chopped
½ pound fresh dates
1 cup vinegar

In a large crock combine all ingredients except the dates and the 1 cup vinegar. Stone the dates, chop them, and cook in the 1 cup vinegar until soft. Then mash well and add to the remaining ingredients. Stir to combine thoroughly, pack in a wide-mouthed jar, cover tightly, and store in a cool place. Serve with all kinds of dishes and *kababs*.

PICKLED APPLES
(*Torshi Sib*)

Cut off ¼-inch slice from the top of the apples and reserve. Remove cores and stuff each apple with a mixture of salt, black pepper, and powdered mint leaves. Replace tops on apples and secure with toothpicks. Pack apples in a large crock and cover with vinegar. Cover tightly and keep at room temperature. Serve with meat and soups.

EGGPLANT PICKLES
(*Torshi Bademjan*)

The most popular pickle in Iran, the one served with every kind of food and at every meal, is made of eggplant. An inordinate craving for this pickle by Persian women is usually associated with much laughter and merriment, for it is accepted proof of pregnancy! I understand that in America the popular dill pickle has much the same amusing connotation.

Several different varieties are made in different parts of the country. Here are two variations:

One: Cut the stem end from 2 large eggplants and make slits about 2 inches deep in the bottoms. Bake the eggplants in a hot oven (400°) until they are well cooked and soft. Then chop and mix the eggplants with 2 tablespoons dry mustard and 1 tablespoon mustard seeds, 2 tablespoons black pepper, ½ teaspoon red pepper, ¼ cup toasted coriander seeds, 3 small hot peppers, 1 tablespoon cardamom, 1 tablespoon chopped ginger root, 2 tablespoons fennel seeds, 1 tablespoon anise seeds, 2 large bulbs of garlic, peeled and chopped, and 1 table-spoon turmeric. Then soak ½ pound tamarind pods in 2 cups strong vinegar. When well soaked, rub with the fingers until the pulp from the pods is mixed smoothly with the vinegar. Strain the mixture into the other ingredients. Add enough vinegar to cover, season with salt to taste, and pack in preserving jars. Cover tightly and store at room temperature.

Two: Cut the stem end from 2 large eggplants and make slits in the bottoms about 3 inches deep. Cover with water in a large pot, bring water to a boil, and simmer until eggplants are very tender. Drain, cut in half, and put in a large sieve to drain for about 2 hours. Then spread the eggplants on a towel and put in a warm place or in the sun to dry completely. The dried eggplant will keep for almost 2 years, ready to be mixed with spices and vinegar for pickles. To make pickle, stuff the inside of half a dried eggplant with the same spices as used in the recipe above. Cover with another half eggplant and place in a crock or jar with vinegar to cover. Serve in a few days.

Beverages

There are two kinds of refreshing drinks served in Persia which are as old as the country itself. One is an uncooked drink made of sugar, water, and the juice of fruit or flowers, served with ice, and called *afshoreh*. The other, made of a cooked mixture of sugar and fruit juices, is known as *sharbat,* or sherbet in English.

Like preserves, all sherbets are made into a fine, clear fruit syrup which may be kept in tightly corked glass bottles for months.

CHERRY SHERBET
(*Alu Balu Sharbat*)

Boil 1 pound fresh sour cherries with 1 cup water in an enamel saucepan until very soft. Mash and filter the liquid through a fine cloth, pressing the cherries gently until all the juice is extracted. Boil 2 pounds sugar (4 cups), dissolved in 1 cup water, for about 3 minutes, or until syrup is clear and sugar is dissolved. Stir in juice. If mixture is too sweet, add lemon juice or citric acid mixed with a little water. Boil until the syrup is almost as thick as maple syrup, but not thick enough to spin a thread. Remove from fire, cool, and pour into sterilized bottles. Cork and store in a cool, dry place.

To serve any sherbet, pour 2 or 3 tablespoons of the fruit syrup into a large glass, add fresh cold water and 1 or 2 ice cubes, if the weather is hot. American palates might prefer adding soda water.

The juice of pomegranates, barberries, rhubarb, sour oranges, verjuice, lemons, or any other sour fruit may be used in place of the cherry juice.

QUINCE AND LIME SHERBET
(*Beh Limu Sharbat*)

This sherbet has medicinal uses in Persia aside from the fact that it is served as a refreshing drink in hot weather.

Peel 1 large ripe quince and drop it into 2 cups water mixed with 3 tablespoons lemon juice. Roll the quince in the acidulated water, round and round, until all sides are thoroughly bathed. This prevents the quince from darkening. Peel another quince, place it in the lemon-juice water, and remove the first one to be grated. Grate both quinces fine, place in a sieve, and press gently to remove as much of the juice as possible. Mix the juice with ½ cup lemon juice. Boil 2 pound sugar (4 cups), dissolved in 1 cup water, to a thick syrup. Add juice and continue to boil until the syrup is thick. Cool and bottle.

SEKANJABIN

This is an ancient health drink which is still well known and enjoyed by every Persian. It is deliciously refreshing in the hot summer and a popular punch to serve with *kababs* and *polous* when mixed with finely grated cucumber. It frequently serves as a light meal, accompanied by romaine and bread.

The leaves of lettuce are folded one by one and dipped into this sherbet. Formerly people affected with jaundice existed almost solely on *sekanjabin* and romaine, but without bread, until their ailment was cured.

Boil 2 cups sugar and 1 cup water until thick, but not thick enough to spin a thread. Add ½ cup white vinegar and the juice of 2 large lemons. Continue to boil until drops of the syrup drip slowly from the end of a spoon. Add a bunch of fresh mint leaves and cook for 3 minutes longer. Strain syrup from the mint, cool, and bottle. If fresh mint leaves are not available use 2 or 3 drops of mint extract.

SEKANJABIN PUNCH

During my visit to California I tried this refreshment on several different occasions, and always with great edification. None of my guests was content with one cup, but always asked for more.

Peel and grate ½ small slender, seeded cucumber into a glass or small bowl with 3 tablespoons *sekanjabin*. Add 2 ice cubes and 2 or 3 crushed almonds and fill glass with ice water.

AFSHOREH
(*Persian Lemonade*)

In olden days *afshorehs* were served with meals, as American coffee is today. At the present time they are served only as mid-meal refreshments. The juices of fruits and extracts of aromatic flowers, seeds, and citrus peels are used to make these beverages.

AFSHOREH LIMU

In a large wineglass combine the juice of one lemon, 1 tablespoon sugar, and 2 ice cubes. Fill glass with water.

ROSE-WATER AFSHOREH

In a glass combine 1 tablespoon sugar and 2 tablespoons rose-flower water or orange-blossom water. Add ice cubes and fill glass with water.

ORANGE-FLOWER AFSHOREH

Soak 1 pound sugar in 1 cup distilled extract of orange or lemon blossoms in a tightly covered container for 2 days. Then put about 2 tablespoons of the syrup in a glass. Add ice cubes and fill glass with water.

VIOLET AFSHOREH
(*Gol Benafsheh*)

Bring 2 cups water to a boil. Add 8 ounces mashed small fresh wild violets, cover tightly, remove from heat, and let stand for 12 hours. Strain liquid from the violets into a measuring cup and add an equal amount of sugar to the flowers.

Return the liquid to the violets and sugar and put in the top of a double boiler. Cook over simmering water until the sugar is completely dissolved. Cool and bottle. Store in a cool, dry place. Serve a small amount of it as *afshoreh,* or without water as violet tea. It is believed to be relaxing to the nerves and mind.

Ancient Health Notes from Persia

Certain well-known foods, herbs, and beverages are believed by the Persians to promote health and well-being.

To what extent the efficacy of these beliefs is based on medical or scientific fact is not really important. The important factor is that certain Persian concepts of food that once may have seemed to be based on superstition are still practiced in Persia, as practical observances of the basic laws of mental and physical health.

Perhaps a knowledge of the century-old health-food habits of my people will help the Western world to have more appreciation and understanding of the ancient culture of Persia.

Throughout the ages the answer to the question of longer-lasting youth and vital health has been yogurt, and many of the earliest records of ancient Persia abound with references to this important milk food. Today it is a well-known fact that yogurt is one of the most easily assimilated protein foods, which releases the Vitamin B stored in the body for use within the digestive system and promotes energy and mental health. In Persia it is used both as a food and a medicine. As a medicine, it is the only nourishment given to one suffering from dysentery or diarrhea.

Mixed with a good quantity of finely chopped fresh garlic, yogurt is one of the oldest cures for malaria, and in most villages and small towns in Persia garlic-infused yogurt is used ex-

tensively as an antidote and preventative for many other illnesses.

Two fresh greens, spinach and coriander, are believed to
revitalize the liver and correct constipation. Coriander, especially, is used extensively in the food of patients and conva-
lescents. For a severe cold the patient is given a thick soup
(*aash*) of rice and chicken to which is added onion and a large
quantity of fresh spinach and coriander. A similar soup, but
containing turnips, is recommended for the patient with a fever
due to a cold virus. And a cure for a cold in the head is the
inhalation of the steam from a big bowl of hot turnips.

Kateh polou mixed with yogurt is a favorite meal for patients
recovering from a severe bout of diarrhea, and most of the
variations of the sour-fruit *khoreshes,* made without meat and
spices, are the main dishes served to one recovering from
dysentery, high blood pressure, or liver conditions. They are
usually served with *kateh* or plain *dami*.

Again for those with digestive grievances a thick pomegranate soup is excellent. This is made by simmering a little rice
and a small bunch of crushed fresh mint leaves in 2 cups of
fresh pomegranate juice.

When verjuice is substituted for the pomegranate juice, the
soup, along with cooked spinach and coriander, is believed to
be helpful to those suffering from rheumatism, arthritis, or
high blood pressure. Other variations of the sour *aashes,* included in the soup chapter, are popular aids for bile disturbances.

Another important health food is Persian bread. It is made
in a long, flat piece as thick as cardboard. In the cities bakery
shops are on every street. Each shop has its round-bellied clay
oven, lined with pebbles and heated with wood. The dough is
flattened over a large, wooden mold with a handle up to approximately 35 inches long, 20 to 25 inches wide and 1 inch
thick. The mold is carried into the oven and the strip of dough

is placed against the side of the oven over the hot pebbles. In this manner it bubbles and browns on both sides, becoming crisp with no soft dough in the center. The bread is usually served fresh and hot from the bakery.

Together with this bread a most healthful and delicious breakfast consists of white cheese mixed with crushed, toasted walnuts and powdered dried wild marjoram and tea and hot milk. With its bitter, pungent taste, wild marjoram is famous for its carminative effect on the digestive system. Bread and white cheese mixed with walnuts and fresh mint leaves are also served for lunch or dinner during the hot days of summer. They are served with grapes or any kind of melon—watermelon, muskmelon, or cantaloupe. This combination of foods is considered nutritious and invigorating. Even Bos-hac refers to it:

> Enjoy bread and muskmelon, not only one,
> But two, three, four, five and six!
> Have them with cheese and walnut, not only one,
> But two, three, four, five and six!

A few other health-food tips from ancient Persian medicine are that by substituting walnuts for red meat a person is made gentle and kind; that plenty of dried red grapes before breakfast improve the memory; lots of pistachios enrich the blood, and citron-peel preserve is a sure cure for anemia.

In early days, long before the drinking of tea became customary, the Persians brewed tisanes from flowers. These flower teas are still considered healthful beverages in Iran and are used not only as preventive medicines but to effect certain cures. Saffron-flower tea, served plain or flavored with dried lime, is believed helpful to heart and nerves, having such strong relaxing effects on the nervous system that the drinker can no longer control his laughter when he drinks too much of it!

Many other flowers are gathered, dried, and sold in shops as medicines for strengthening the nerves, heart, brain, and eyes. Popular ones are the flowers of the camomile, the violet, and the hollyhock. Another is a purple flower with large leaves shaped like a cow's tongue called cow tongue, which grows in abundance everywhere in Persia. The dried petals, steamed like tea in a pot, make a beverage drunk daily, sweetened with rock candy. And in many old-fashioned families all these flowers are kept on hand for such emergencies as fainting caused by shock, overwork, heart attack, and other illnesses.

There are men and women in all parts of the country whose job is to collect from the gardeners at the beginning of spring tons of a variety of medicinal flowers, in addition to citrus peels and anise and fennel seeds. These they distill and store in large jars to sell to housewives. The distilled water of citrus peels, especially of citron, also the extracts from anise and fennel are all popularly believed to relieve colic pains and other disturbances of the degestive tract.

Pussy-willow distilled water is believed to have a strengthening effect on the heart. Pussy-willow flower, called *Beed Meshk,* or musk of willow, grows in many parts of Iran. The flowers, three inches long and about one inch wide, are covered with a feathery gray hair. The distilled aromatic water of this flower must be drunk about two hours after breakfast or two hours before lunch. It is frequently sweetened with sugar and served iced.

Another, and perhaps the most important food fact which the Persians have known for centuries, and which is today certainly more fact than fiction, is that an excess of fat in the diet causes liver and heart ailments and produces hardening of the arteries. Ancient Persian physicians found a natural way to counteract the storing up of excess fats within the body. They believed that eating the sour juices and vinegars or fruits with their foods would neutralize the fat. As a result, all sorts of sour juices are used in Persian dishes, especially in fried foods and other dishes with any quantity of fat, and innumerable varieties of sour pickles are placed on the table to be enjoyed with every meal.

Seven hundred years ago, in the end of his *Divan*, Bos-hac said:

"Oh I pray thee wayfarer, if ever you pass my humble grave
With an utterance, sweet as Halva, pray make my soul happy."

And so say I.

—The End—

English Index

Persian Index

THE HIPPOCRENE COOKBOOK LIBRARY

Persian Dictionaries and Language Guides from Hippocrene …

PERSIAN-ENGLISH STANDARD DICTIONARY
22,500 entries • 0-7818-0055-2 • $19.95p • (350)

ENGLISH-PERSIAN STANDARD DICTIONARY
40,000 entries • 0-7818-0056-0 • $19.95p • (367)

**FARSI-ENGLISH/ENGLISH-FARSI (PERSIAN)
CONCISE DICTIONARY**
8,400 entries • 0-7818-0860-X • $12.95p • (260)

**FARSI-ENGLISH/ENGLISH-FARSI DICTIONARY &
PHRASEBOOK, ROMANIZED**
4,000 entries • 0-7818-1073-6 • $11.95p • (367)

BEGINNER'S PERSIAN
0-7818-0567-8 • $14.95p • (696)

BEGINNER'S DARI (PERSIAN)
0-7818-1012-4 • $16.95p • (233)

All prices subject to change. To purchase Hippocrene Books contact your local bookstore, call (718) 454-2366, or write to: HIPPOCRENE BOOKS, 171 Madison Avenue, New York, NY 10016. Please enclose check or money order, adding $5.00 shipping (UPS) for the first book and $.50 for each additional book.

www.ingramcontent.com/pod-product-compliance
Lightning Source LLC
Jackson TN
JSHW011401130125
77033JS00023B/788

* 9 7 8 0 7 8 1 8 0 2 4 1 3 *